BEHIND THE MUSK

BY MARTIN MBURU KABECHA

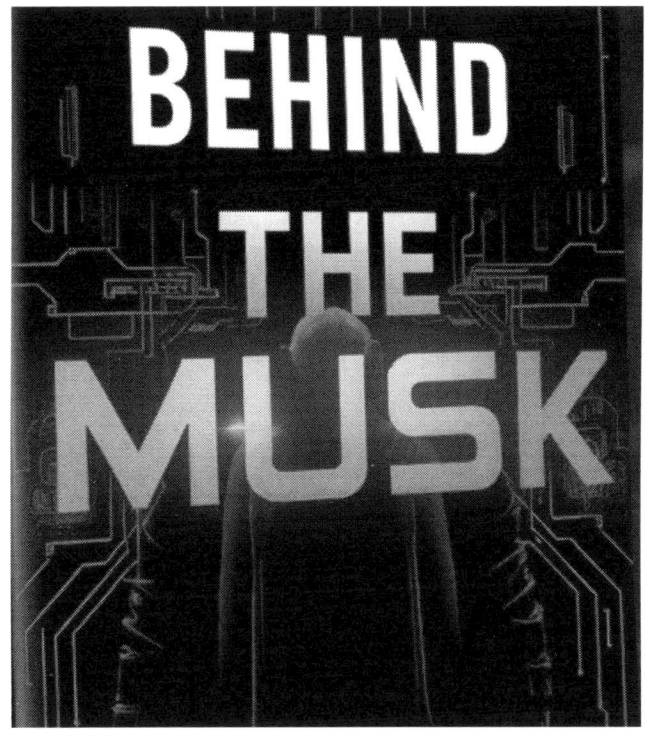

CHAPTER ONE
Disconnected Connections

Social Media Pressure and Authentic Friendships

In today's digital age, where social media is often the center of social lives, many young people find themselves trapped in a world of likes, followers, and filtered images. Social media has become a platform for connection and a source of pressure to present a "perfect" version of oneself. This chapter explores the impact of social media on personal identity and relationships, significantly how it often blurs the line between genuine friendships and virtual connections.

The story follows Sophia, a high school student who bases her self-worth on the number of likes and comments she receives online. As she becomes more invested in her digital persona, she starts feeling isolated and disconnected from the people around her. She realizes her friendships lack depth, which is more about maintaining an online image than fostering genuine connection. Through her journey, Sophia learns the importance of authenticity, balancing her digital presence, and developing meaningful, face-to-face relationships beyond the screen. This chapter highlights the power of genuine connection and the need to prioritize real friendships over superficial online validation.

Sophia sat on her bed, her phone lighting up her face in the darkened room. Her fingers scrolled through Instagram, Twitter, and Snapchat, flicking past dozens of posts and stories. She was mesmerized, lost in the carefully curated lives of people she barely knew. Influencers, classmates, and strangers seemed to be living incredible lives. In comparison, her life felt bland and uninspired.

Her own Instagram feed was an art she had perfected. Her pictures were vibrant and filtered to perfection. The captions were witty and carefully crafted to capture just the right amount of interest without trying too hard. And the likes—oh, the likes—were the validation she craved. Each heart that appeared on her posts felt like a small pat on the back, a subtle reminder that she mattered.

But tonight felt different. As she scrolled through her feed, an unsettling feeling crept into her mind. All her friends—at least, those she called her "friends" online—looked happy, vibrant, and full of life. They were hanging out together, posting stories of laughter, movie nights, and late-night snacks. And Sophia was in none of them.

It wasn't that she hadn't been invited. She had been invited to the movie night that was now all over her friends' stories. But she decided to stay home at the last minute, telling them she was too tired. In reality, she had just wanted to spend the night scrolling through social media, feeling the comfort of her room hidden behind the screen. It was easier and safer. She didn't have to worry about awkward silences or saying the wrong thing.

As she lay there, scrolling through other people's seemingly perfect lives, Sophia felt something shift. She felt... empty. She tried to shake it off, dismissing it as a passing feeling, but it lingered. She closed her eyes, trying to ignore the faint ache in her chest, but the feeling grew more assertive. She wanted more than likes, comments, and emojis. She wanted real connections—friendships that didn't rely on a screen to exist.

Sophia noticed how detached she felt as she walked through the school hallways the next day. Her "friends" waved at her, exchanged casual "hellos," and then moved on, each absorbed in their lives. They weren't bad friends, but their connections felt superficial, almost as if they only existed within the confines of a digital screen.

As the week wore on, Sophia became more aware of how her social media use affected her life. She spent hours scrolling without realizing it, often to the point of exhaustion. She would go to bed late, her mind filled with images and stories of other people's lives, unable to find peace. Her real-world friendships felt dull and uninspired, almost like she was living two separate lives—one online and one offline. And the online version was taking up more space.

It wasn't until Friday night that she finally hit her breaking point. She was supposed to go to a small party with her friends, but instead, she sat at her vanity, staring at her reflection and feeling utterly lost. She picked up her phone, ready to scroll through social media again when a thought struck her: *What if I just put it down? What if I went and connected with my friends without worrying about capturing the perfect photo or finding the right angle?*

Taking a deep breath, Sophia put her phone in her drawer and left it there. No notifications, no selfies, no constant scrolling. She walked out the door without her phone for the first time in a long time, feeling nervous but exhilarated. She felt exposed and vulnerable but accessible in a way she hadn't in months.

At the party, she was quiet at first, unsure how to engage without the comfort of her phone. Her friends were surprised to see her so present, so focused on them. Instead of checking her screen every few seconds, she listened, laughed, and shared stories. She felt the warmth of laughter and the joy of genuine connection, free from the pressure to document every moment.

Later, as they sat around a fire in the backyard, Sophia finally shared her feelings. She told them about her emptiness, the pressure to be perfect online, and how it took over her life. To her surprise, her friends understood. They nodded, sharing their stories of feeling overwhelmed by social media and comparing their lives to the unrealistic standards they saw on their screens.

They spent hours talking about everything—real, honest conversations that went beyond emojis and hashtags. They laughed about their quirks, shared insecurities, and revealed parts of themselves they'd kept hidden. Sophia realized her friends weren't as perfect as their online personas suggested. They were just like her—flawed, uncertain, and sometimes struggling to find their way.

At that moment, she felt a more profound connection than any like or comment could provide. It was raw, unfiltered, and honest.

As she returned home the following day, Sophia felt like a weight had been lifted from her shoulders. She didn't need to live up to a social media version of herself anymore, and she didn't need the likes or the comments to feel validated. She realized that her followers or her feed didn't define her worth. Her value came from being present, connecting with the people around her, and embracing her authentic self.

From that day on, Sophia consciously decided to limit her time on social media. She still enjoyed sharing moments, but now, she did it mindfully. She no longer needed the constant validation of strangers. She invested her time building meaningful, face-to-face relationships and enjoying the world beyond her screen.

Sophia's journey taught her an invaluable lesson: life happens in real time, not in the filtered images on her phone. She learned to cherish her friends, moments, and herself—unfiltered, raw, and completely real.

The screen may have been a comforting escape, but it was no substitute for the genuine connections she found when she put her phone down and looked up at the world around her.

CHAPTER TWO
The Grades Game

Academic Pressure and Mental Health

Academic success is the gateway to future achievements for many students, leading to intense pressure to perform and maintain high grades. This chapter delves into academic pressure, exploring how the constant drive to excel can affect a student's mental health and overall well-being.

The story follows Liam, a high-achieving student who feels the weight of expectations from his family, teachers, and even himself. Determined to maintain his perfect GPA, he sacrifices sleep, hobbies, and social connections, gradually spiraling into burnout and anxiety. As the stress builds, he begins to realize that his pursuit of academic perfection is costing him his mental health. Through guidance from his school counselor, Liam learns that his worth isn't defined solely by his grades. He discovers strategies for managing stress, setting realistic goals, and prioritizing self-care, ultimately embracing a healthier approach to learning. This chapter emphasizes the importance of mental health and balance, encouraging students to pursue academic success without sacrificing well-being.

Liam was known as "the smart kid." He'd been at the top of his class since elementary school, and everyone expected him to stay that way. His teachers praised him, his friends admired him, and his parents had high hopes for his future. But with each new year of high school, the pressure grew more intense. Every test, every assignment, and every project felt like it could make or break his future. He had to be perfect. Or so he thought.

As the junior year began, Liam's schedule was packed. Honors courses, AP classes, extracurricular activities, and endless homework consumed his days and nights. It wasn't long before the pressure started weighing him down. He stayed up late every night, sometimes sleeping only four or five hours, to keep up with his workload. Caffeine became his best friend and carried an ever-present, lingering worry that he wasn't doing enough.

One afternoon, his history teacher returned an essay they had submitted the previous week. Liam's heart raced as he saw his grade —a B+. It felt like a punch to the gut. He'd worked hard on that essay, spending hours researching and perfecting every sentence, but it still wasn't enough. It wasn't an A. He felt like he had failed.

"Are you okay?" his friend Mira asked, noticing his sullen expression.

"Yeah, I'm fine," he replied quickly, shoving the paper into his backpack. But inside, he was anything but delicate. He felt like he was slipping and was terrified of letting anyone down—his teachers, parents, himself.

That night, as he sat at his desk staring at another mountain of homework, he couldn't focus. The words on the page blurred, and his mind was spinning with worries. *What if I don't get into a good college? What if I disappoint everyone?* His heart pounded, his hands shook, and a knot of anxiety tightened in his chest.

He closed his books, leaned back, and stared at the ceiling. He felt like he was drowning. He couldn't remember the last time he felt happy or at ease. School, once a place of excitement and learning, had become a source of stress and anxiety.

The next day, Liam visited the school counselor's office for the first time. He wasn't even sure why he'd gone—maybe he just needed someone to talk to, someone who wouldn't judge him or expect him to be perfect. Mrs. Kim, the counselor, greeted him with a warm smile.

"Hi, Liam. How can I help you?" she asked gently.

Liam hesitated, unsure of where to begin. He took a deep breath. "I... I'm just feeling overwhelmed. With school, grades... everything."

Mrs. Kim nodded, listening intently as Liam explained his pressure to be the best and never make mistakes. "It feels like if I'm not perfect, I'm failing," he admitted, his voice barely a whisper.

"Liam," Mrs. Kim said softly, "it sounds like you're carrying a heavy burden. Sometimes, we put so much pressure on ourselves that we forget to take care of our mental health. It's okay to want to succeed, but giving yourself grace is also important."

They spent the rest of the session discussing his worries, his fear of failure, and the unrealistic expectations he had set for himself. Mrs. Kim suggested strategies to help him manage his stress, such as taking short breaks, setting boundaries for study time, and practicing mindfulness to calm his racing thoughts.

At first, Liam was skeptical. How could taking breaks or breathing exercises help him get an A? But he decided to give it a try. Over the next few weeks, he incorporated these strategies into his routine. When he felt his anxiety building up, he would take a few deep breaths, close his eyes, and try to ground himself in the present moment. He started going for short walks to clear his mind and took breaks when he felt overwhelmed.

Gradually, he began to notice a difference. The anxiety was still there, but it felt more manageable. He was learning to be kinder to himself, to accept that he didn't need to be perfect. And he realized something important: his grades didn't define him.

One afternoon, as he studied for an upcoming chemistry test, he felt the familiar wave of anxiety rising. His mind started racing with worst-case scenarios, but he paused, took a deep breath, and reminded himself that he was doing his best—and his best was enough.

When he got his test back a week later, he had scored an A-. It wasn't a perfect score, but for the first time, Liam didn't feel disappointed. He felt proud. He was proud of the effort he had put in, the resilience he was building, and himself for not letting the pressure consume him.

Liam continued meeting with Mrs. Kim, who helped him set realistic goals and reminded him that mental health was as important as academic success. He also opened up to his parents, sharing his struggles with them. They were surprised but supportive and assured him they loved him regardless of his grades.

Over time, Liam learned to find a balance. He still worked hard and cared about his grades, but he also made time for himself—time to relax, enjoy hobbies, and spend time with friends. He even joined the school's mindfulness club, meeting other students with similar pressures. They shared their stories, supported one another, and discovered they were not alone in their struggles.

By the end of junior year, Liam had transformed his school approach. He still had moments of stress and anxiety, but he had the tools to handle them. He had learned that success wasn't about being perfect or achieving straight A's. Success was about doing his best, taking care of himself, and finding joy in learning.

Liam's journey taught him that life is more than grades and achievements. It's about resilience, self-compassion, and growth. And as he looked forward to his senior year, he knew he had the strength to face whatever challenges came his way.

He was no longer just "the smart kid." He was Liam—capable, resilient, and ready to embrace the journey ahead.

CHAPTER THREE
Identity Crisis

Self-Discovery and Gender Identity

High school is often a time of exploration and self-discovery. Still, understanding who one is can be particularly complex for some students, especially regarding gender identity questions. This chapter addresses the journey of self-acceptance and the courage it takes to embrace one's true self in a world filled with labels, expectations, and societal pressures.

In this story, we follow Avery, a student grappling with their gender identity and feeling pressured to fit into society's predefined boxes. Surrounded by family, friends, and schoolmates who may not fully understand, Avery feels isolated and unsure of how to navigate this personal journey. With the support of a compassionate teacher and a group of understanding peers, Avery learns to embrace their identity authentically. This chapter highlights the importance of self-discovery, acceptance, and creating supportive, inclusive environments where everyone feels safe to be themselves. It encourages readers to respect and support others on their unique journeys and reminds them that authenticity is a source of strength.

Avery stood in front of the bathroom mirror, staring at their reflection. The person looking back was a puzzle, each piece unfamiliar and out of place. It felt as if they were looking at a stranger. At school, at home, and even with friends, they felt this unshakeable weight pressing down on them. They were playing a role in a play they hadn't signed up for, forced to recite lines that didn't feel like their own.

At school, Avery often felt boxed in. There were unspoken rules about how they were supposed to act, dress, and even talk. Boys were expected to act tough, play sports, and laugh off emotions. Girls were expected to look a certain way, talk a certain way, and fit into the mold of femininity. But Avery didn't feel like they fit into either category.

The pressure to conform came from everywhere—family, friends, even strangers who barely knew them. Their parents loved them, but they had a picture-perfect vision of who they thought Avery was supposed to be. They'd pick out clothes for Avery, always choosing items they thought were "appropriate" for a boy or girl, but Avery couldn't shake the discomfort each time they slipped into something that didn't feel right. It was like a costume, covering up who they indeed were.

Their teacher, Ms. Carson, noticed Avery's quiet in English class. She had a gift for sensing when her students were struggling and made it a point to create a safe classroom environment. One day, as the class read The Catcher in the Rye, she assigned a personal essay. The prompt was simple but powerful: "Who are you?"

That night, Avery sat at their desk, staring at a blank piece of paper, feeling the question's weight. *Who am I?* They didn't know the answer. They'd spent so much time trying to be what others expected that they weren't sure who they were anymore.

The words didn't come quickly, but slowly, Avery started writing. They wrote about feeling like they didn't belong, about the expectations that felt suffocating, about wanting to break free from labels. They poured out their fears, confusion, and desire to find a place to be themselves and not have to fit into any predefined role.

They felt exposed when they turned in their essays, as if they'd peeled back a layer of themselves and laid it bare. They weren't sure if it was the right thing to do, but they trusted Ms. Carson. She always seemed to understand things about her students that others overlooked.

A few days later, Ms. Carson asked Avery to stay after class. She sat down beside them, holding the essay in her hands. Her eyes were kind and understanding.

"Avery," she began, "your essay moved me. You have a lot of courage to share what you did. I want you to know that it's okay to feel different and it's okay to take your time figuring out who you are. You're not alone in this."

Avery felt a wave of relief wash over them. Hearing those words —"you're not alone"—was like a lifeline in the middle of a storm. Ms. Carson told them about a support group at school called the GSA (Gender and Sexuality Alliance). In this judgment-free environment, students could talk openly about their identities. She encouraged Avery to attend, promising it was a safe space where they could be themselves.

Nervous but curious, Avery decided to go. When they walked into the room for the first time, they were greeted by students from all backgrounds, each carrying their own stories and struggles. Some were like Avery, unsure of where they fit in, while others had already embraced their identities. There was laughter, conversation, and an atmosphere of acceptance that Avery hadn't felt in a long time.

They sat in a circle, and one by one, the students shared their journeys, triumphs, and challenges. When it was Avery's turn, they hesitated initially, unsure how to express their feelings. But as they looked around the room, at the faces of people who were listening and genuinely cared, they found the courage to speak.

"I... I'm not sure who I am," Avery admitted, their voice trembling. "I feel like I'm supposed to fit into a box, but I don't. I don't want to be someone I'm not, but it's hard when everyone expects you to be a certain way."

The students nodded, their eyes filled with empathy and understanding. They'd all been there at some point, caught between society's expectations and their true selves. A student named Alex, who identified as nonbinary, shared their own story of self-discovery and the challenges they'd faced along the way.

"It's okay not to have all the answers," Alex said. "The important thing is to be true to yourself, even if it's scary. We're all here to support each other."

Avery attended the GSA meetings regularly, and each session felt like a step closer to finding themselves. They experimented with their appearance, trying clothes and styles that felt comfortable and true to their identity. They started to learn more about gender identity and realized that they didn't have to fit into any one label—they could define themselves on their terms.

Over time, Avery found the courage to open up to their friends. They shared their journey, their fears, and the joy they felt in discovering who they were. Their friends were supportive, even if they didn't fully understand. What mattered was that they respected Avery's journey and were there for them.

The real test came when Avery decided to talk to their parents. It was a difficult conversation, filled with emotions and uncertainty. At first, their parents were confused, worried that they'd done something wrong or that Avery was going through a "phase." But with patience and honesty, Avery explained that this was who they were and that this journey wasn't about defying anyone's expectations but about embracing their true self.

It took time, but eventually, Avery's parents began to understand. They didn't have all the answers and made mistakes along the way, but they were willing to listen and learn. They even attended a support group for parents, determined to support Avery in every way possible.

With each step, Avery's confidence grew. They felt more comfortable in their skin and more at ease with the person they were becoming. They realized that identity wasn't a box to fit into—it was a journey, a uniquely their path. Along the way, they'd found people who loved and supported them for who they were, not for who society thought they should be.

By the end of the school year, Avery felt a sense of peace they hadn't felt before. They'd understand that self-discovery wasn't about conforming to others' expectations. It was about looking inward, embracing their authentic self, and surrounding themselves with people who accepted them unconditionally.

As Avery walked through the school hallways, they no longer felt like strangers in their own lives. They were Avery—brave, unique, and true to themselves. And for the first time, they knew that was enough.

CHAPTER FOUR
Digital Detox

Smartphone Addiction and Mindfulness

In a world where smartphones and digital devices have become constant companions, many young people find themselves tethered to screens, often at the expense of real-life experiences and mental well-being. This chapter explores the theme of smartphone addiction and the benefits of practicing mindfulness, encouraging readers to find a healthier balance with technology.

The story centers around Max, a high school student constantly connected to his phone—scrolling through social media, texting friends, and playing games. He starts to notice that his attention span is dwindling, his grades are slipping, and he's missing out on meaningful moments with friends and family. Realizing the impact of his digital dependence, Max decides to take on the challenge of a "digital detox." With the support of his friends, he sets boundaries for his screen time and engages in mindfulness activities, such as meditation, nature walks, and journaling. Through his journey, Max learns to appreciate the world beyond his screen, discovering the joy of being present and connected to his surroundings. This chapter encourages readers to practice mindful living, showing that life can be more prosperous and fulfilling when they take breaks from constant digital distractions.

Max's phone buzzed as he lay in bed, barely awake. His hand instinctively reached for it, his fingers swiping open the screen before his eyes were fully open. Instagram, Snapchat, TikTok—he had notifications from everywhere. Messages, comments, likes—a whirlwind of digital noise greeted him every morning.

It had become his routine: wake up, scroll through notifications, check his social media feeds, and dive headfirst into the digital world before he even left his bed. It was comforting to see what everyone else was up to, catch the latest memes, and stay connected with his friends. But it was also exhausting, and lately, Max had started to notice something: the more he scrolled, the more tired he felt. And the more tired he felt, the more he scrolled. It was a cycle he couldn't seem to break.

At school, it was the same. Between classes, he'd be on his phone, earbuds in, scrolling mindlessly through his feed, rarely looking up or talking to the people around him. During lunch, he'd sit with his friends, but most of them would be doing the same thing—heads down, eyes on their screens, fingers tapping and swiping. They were together, but they were all in their little worlds.

One day, as he sat in math class, he zoned out, his mind drifting as he stared at the clock, counting down the minutes until he could recheck his phone. When the bell finally rang, he felt excited as he reached for his phone, but it felt... empty. He couldn't remember anything the teacher had discussed in class. It was like he hadn't been there at all.

That night, as he lay in bed, scrolling through Instagram for the hundredth time, he came across a post from an influencer he followed. It was a picture of her hiking in a beautiful forest, with the caption: *"Taking a break from screens and finding peace in the real world. Digital detox complete!"*

The words stuck with him. A digital detox? The idea seemed strange—why would anyone want to go without their phone? But as he thought about it, he realized he hadn't been present in his life for a long time. It was like he lived through a screen, experiencing life in little snapshots instead of being there.

The following day, he woke up and made a decision. He was going to try a digital detox. Just for a week. No social media, no mindless scrolling, no constant checking of notifications. He didn't know if he could do it, but he felt he had to try.

Max told his friends about his plan at lunch to hold himself accountable. At first, they laughed. "Good luck with that, Max," his friend Jordan teased. "You're practically glued to that thing."

But his friend Lily looked intrigued. "That sounds cool. I've felt the same way lately; I'm missing out on real life. Maybe I'll try it with you."

Max was surprised but glad to have a partner in this challenge. They both put their phones on silent and slipped them into their backpacks, promising each other that they wouldn't check them until the end of the school day.

At first, it felt strange. Every time there was a lull in conversation, Max's hand would automatically reach for his pocket, only to find it empty. He felt a pang of anxiety, like he was missing something important. But as the day went on, he felt a little lighter, as if a weight had been lifted from his shoulders.

Over the next few days, Max and Lily continued their digital detox, and the effects were more potent than they had expected. Instead of staring at their screens during lunch, they talked—talked. They laughed, shared stories, and listened to each other. Without the distraction of their phones, they noticed things they hadn't before, such as how their friends' eyes lit up when they talked about something they were passionate about, the sound of laughter echoing through the cafeteria, and the feeling of being fully present.

Max joined Lily for a walk in the park after school one afternoon. Without his phone, he noticed the world around him in a way he hadn't in a long time. He felt the sun's warmth on his face, heard the rustling of leaves, and smelled the fresh, earthy scent of the trees. It was peaceful and calming, and he felt a sense of connection to the world he hadn't felt in a long time.

As the week went on, Max started practicing mindfulness, something he'd learned about from a YouTube video (which he ironically had watched during his screen time). Every morning, he'd take a few minutes to sit silently, focusing on breathing and calming his mind. At first, it felt strange and uncomfortable, but he found it helped him feel more grounded and centered over time.

One evening, he sat with his parents at dinner and put his phone in another room. Usually, he'd eat with one hand while scrolling with the other, barely paying attention to the conversation. But that night, he listened as his mom talked about her day, and his dad told a funny story about a coworker. He laughed, genuinely enjoyed the moment, and felt closer to them than he had in a long time.

By the end of the week, Max felt like a different person. He wasn't constantly reaching for his phone and didn't feel the same urge to check his notifications every five minutes. He felt accessible, present, and connected to the world around him.

On the last day of his digital detox, he decided to recheck his social media, but he did it mindfully this time. He set a ten-minute timer, scrolled through his feed, liked a few posts, and then put his phone away. He didn't feel the need to keep scrolling, to keep searching for validation. He was content.

At school, his friends noticed the change in him. "You seem different, Max," Jordan said one day. "Like... happier. What's your secret?"

Max smiled. "I just realized there's more to life than what's on a screen. I was missing out on everything around me because I was so focused on what everyone else was doing. Taking a break helped me see what matters."

From that day on, Max maintained a healthier relationship with his phone. He still used social media but didn't let it consume him. He made time for what brought him absolute joy: spending time with friends, being outdoors, and practicing mindfulness.

The digital detox had been a challenge, but it taught him an invaluable lesson: life was happening all around him, and he didn't need a screen to feel connected. He just needed to look up and be present.

Max's journey reminded him that technology is a tool, not a way of life. With a bit of balance, he can enjoy the best of both worlds: staying connected to his friends online while truly experiencing the world around him.

Ultimately, Max learned that sometimes, disconnecting is the best way to stay connected. That was a lesson worth remembering.

CHAPTER FIVE
Bully in the DMs

Cyberbullying and Self-Worth

As social media and online interactions become a big part of daily life, cyberbullying has emerged as a significant issue for many teens. This chapter addresses the challenges of dealing with cyberbullying, its impact on self-esteem, and the journey toward resilience and self-worth.

The story follows Riley, a creative student who loves sharing her art online. At first, she finds joy and encouragement from her followers, but soon, anonymous messages appear, filled with harsh criticism and hurtful words. The negativity starts to weigh on her, eroding her confidence and making her question her passion. Riley becomes withdrawn, fearful of putting herself out there again. With the help of her close friends and a supportive teacher, she learns strategies to cope with cyberbullying, such as blocking and reporting harassers, focusing on positive feedback, and reminding herself of her value beyond online comments. Through her journey, Riley discovers the importance of resilience, self-compassion, and believing in herself regardless of others' opinions. This chapter highlights the importance of self-worth and teaches readers that they have the power to stand up to online bullying, seek support, and continue pursuing what they love.

Riley's fingers trembled slightly as she hit "Post." She'd been working on her latest painting for weeks, pouring hours into every tiny detail. The finished piece, a vibrant landscape of mountains against a golden sunset, had made her feel so proud. It was a part of herself, a glimpse into her imagination, and sharing her art online always felt like she was putting a piece of her heart out there for the world to see.

The first comments came in quickly, as they usually did. Friends and family left words of encouragement: *"Amazing work, Riley!" "So talented!" "This is beautiful!"* Each notification brought a warm glow to her heart, reminding her why she loved sharing her art.

But as Riley refreshed the page, she noticed a new comment. Her heart sank as she read it.

"This is terrible. You should give up."

She froze, feeling her heart race. It was an anonymous account with no profile picture and no followers. It's just a blank face and a hurtful message. She tried to brush it off—she told herself it was just one person and didn't mean anything. But as the days passed, the cruel comments didn't stop. Every time she posted something new, the anonymous account was there, leaving comments like *"Amateur work,"* *"This is ugly,"* and *"You have no talent."*

At first, Riley tried to ignore it, but it wasn't that easy. The harsh words stayed with her, replaying in her mind repeatedly. She couldn't help but hear those insults whenever she looked at her art. Her confidence, once so strong, was beginning to crumble. She second-guessed every brushstroke, hesitating before hitting "Post," afraid of what the bully might say next.

Eventually, she stopped sharing her work altogether. Once filled with vibrant colors and detailed designs, her sketchbook began to gather dust on her desk. She spent less time painting, and even her friends noticed the change in her.

"Hey, Riley," her friend Sophie said one day as they sat together in the cafeteria. "You haven't posted any art in a while. What's going on?"

Riley looked down, her cheeks flushing with embarrassment. She didn't want to admit that the words of a faceless stranger were getting to her, but the truth was hard to hide.

"There's… someone leaving mean comments on my posts," Riley mumbled. "They keep saying horrible things about my art, and… I don't know. I feel like maybe they're right."

Sophie frowned, her expression softening with concern. "Riley, don't let one person take away what you love. You're so talented! Those comments are just words from someone who doesn't even know you."

Riley managed a small smile, but the weight in her chest remained. It was easy to say that words didn't matter, but they still hurt.

Later that day, Sophie pulled her aside. "I think you should talk to Ms. Evans," she suggested, referring to their art teacher. "She's been through a lot and always knows what to say. Maybe she can help."

Reluctantly, Riley agreed. She didn't want to bother Ms. Evans but knew she needed to talk to someone deep down.

Ms. Evans welcomed Riley into her office with a warm smile. "What's on your mind, Riley?" she asked gently, noticing the worry in her eyes.

Riley hesitated, then took a deep breath and explained everything — the anonymous comments, the self-doubt, the fear that maybe she wasn't good enough. Ms. Evans listened without interrupting, and her expression was compassionate and understanding.

"Riley," she began softly, "the internet can be a wonderful place, but it can also be harsh. People feel they can say anything behind a screen because they're hidden. But those words? They're just noise. They don't define who you are or your capabilities."

Riley nodded, absorbing her teacher's words.

"And as for this anonymous account, remember, you have control over who can reach you," Ms. Evans continued. "Have you tried reporting or blocking them?"

Riley shook her head. It hadn't even crossed her mind that she had the power to stop the comments from appearing. She'd been so wrapped up in the negativity that she hadn't considered there might be ways to handle it.

Ms. Evans showed her how to report the account, walking her through the steps on her phone. "The online world has tools to protect you," she said. "Blocking, reporting—it's not about running away; it's about standing up for yourself."

With Ms. Evans's help, Riley blocked the anonymous account, taking the first step toward reclaiming her peace of mind.

But Ms. Evans wasn't finished. She suggested something else—an assignment of sorts. "I want you to write down why you love art," she said. "Focus on what makes it meaningful for you. Then, if you're comfortable, I'd like you to share your work with the class next week. Not because of the grades or anyone's opinion, but because art is part of who you are."

Riley left the office feeling lighter, holding onto Ms. Evans's words like a lifeline. That night, she sat at her desk and opened her sketchbook for the first time in days. She started drawing—not for anyone else, not for social media, but for herself. As her pencil moved across the paper, she felt the familiar rush of joy, the sense of creation that had always brought her so much happiness.

When the day came to share her work with the class, Riley felt nervous and determined. She held her sketchbook up, showing her classmates a new piece she'd created—a self-portrait surrounded by vibrant colors, each stroke representing her journey to regain her confidence.

As she explained her work, she noticed her classmates listening intently, their eyes filled with admiration and respect. For the first time, she felt seen, heard, and understood.

When she finished, Sophie and the rest of the class applauded. "This is amazing, Riley!" Sophie said, beaming. "You're so talented, and we're lucky to see your work."

The applause and encouragement filled Riley with a warmth she hadn't felt in weeks. She realized that her faithful supporters, her real friends, were there with her every step of the way. They weren't hiding behind screens, leaving cruel comments. They were present, cheering her on and helping her grow.

From that day on, Riley decided to be kinder to herself. She still loved sharing her art online but did it on her terms. If another negative comment appeared, she knew how to block and report it, and most importantly, she knew that those words didn't define her.

Riley rediscovered her self-worth, not through likes or positive comments, but through the resilience she'd built within herself. She found that her art was her voice, her way of expressing who she was, and no one could take that away from her.

As she continued to create, she no longer sought validation from anonymous faces. Instead, she drew for herself, her friends, and anyone who saw her art and felt a spark of joy. And in doing so, Riley reclaimed her confidence, passion, and love for art.

The bully in the DMs had tried to tear her down, but Riley had emerged stronger. She knew now that her self-worth didn't come from anyone else but from within. And that realization was the greatest masterpiece of all.

CHAPTER SIX
FOMO (Fear of Missing Out)

Social Comparison and Gratitude

In a world where social media constantly showcases the highlights of others' lives, many teens feel a sense of "FOMO"—the Fear of Missing Out. This chapter explores the theme of social comparison, the emotional toll it can take, and the power of gratitude in finding contentment with one's own life.

The story centers around Jessie, a high school student who frequently scrolls through her friends' posts of parties, trips, and seemingly perfect experiences. She begins to feel like she's always missing out as if everyone else lives a more exciting life than hers. The endless comparisons make her anxious and insecure, disconnecting her from her happiness. As Jessie struggles with these feelings, she learns about practicing gratitude from her school counselor. With encouragement, she begins focusing on her unique experiences and finds joy in small moments that make her life meaningful. Through her journey, Jessie learns that social media only shows a curated version of reality and that her life is just as valuable and unique, even if it doesn't look like others. This chapter encourages readers to appreciate their lives and find contentment by focusing on their unique journey rather than comparing themselves to others.

Jessie stared at her phone, scrolling through her Instagram feed with envy. There it was again—the flood of photos from parties, beach trips, and spontaneous adventures that her friends seemed to be having without her. Every swipe brought new snapshots of people laughing, dancing, and living life to the fullest. Each post felt like a reminder of all the things she wasn't doing, all the experiences she was missing out on.

She couldn't shake the feeling of being left behind, like everyone else's lives were moving forward while hers was stuck in place. She saw her friend Lucy at a concert, arms raised in excitement. Another friend, Mia, was at a picnic in the park, laughing with a group of people Jessie barely knew. Even her classmates, who she wasn't particularly close to, seemed to be having the time of their lives.

Jessie set her phone down and sighed, a heavy emptiness settling in her chest. *Why wasn't she invited? Why did it feel like everyone was living a life so much more exciting than hers?*

She'd been invited to some of these events before but usually declined. She was naturally shy and didn't always feel comfortable in big crowds. She preferred quiet nights at home with her books or a movie. But she was seeing the fun everyone else seemed to be having, which made her feel like she was missing out on something essential. Like her life wasn't as colorful or meaningful as theirs.

One afternoon, Jessie sat in her room, scrolling through photos from a beach party she hadn't been invited to. Her heart sank. *Maybe they didn't want her there. Perhaps she was missing out because she wasn't... good enough.* She hated feeling this way, but it was hard not to when social media constantly reminded her of everything she wasn't doing.

Her mom noticed her somber mood and knocked gently on her door. "Hey, Jessie. Is everything okay?"

Jessie hesitated. She didn't want to seem petty or overly dramatic, but she couldn't hide the sadness in her voice. "I just... I feel like I'm missing out. Everyone's out there, having these amazing experiences, and I'm just... here. I'm not doing anything exciting. I'm... boring."

Her mom gave her a sympathetic smile and sat down beside her. "I know it can feel that way sometimes, especially with social media. But remember, what you see online is just a small part of people's lives. It's like the highlight reel. Everyone has ups and downs, but we usually only see the good moments."

Jessie sighed, still feeling the weight of her insecurities. "But it feels like everyone else is living a better life than I am."

Her mom gently touched her shoulder. "It's okay to feel this way. But have you ever tried focusing on what you're grateful for? Sometimes, when we compare ourselves to others, we forget to appreciate the things that make our lives special."

Gratitude. Jessie had heard the word before, but she'd never considered it a way to combat the fear of missing out. She decided to try it to lift the weight off her chest.

That night, Jessie pulled out an empty notebook and wrote at the top of the page: *Things I'm Grateful For.* She paused, her pen hovering over the paper, unsure where to start. Her life didn't seem as exciting as she saw online, but she forced herself to think deeper.

She started small. *My family.* Her parents were kind and supportive, always there when she needed them. She added her cat, Whiskers, who was her constant companion and always curled beside her when she felt lonely. She wrote down her favorite books, which she could lose herself in for hours.

Then she thought about her best friend, Grace. Grace was one of the few people who truly understood her, and they spent countless hours talking about everything from school to dreams for the future. It wasn't flashy or Instagram-worthy, but it was real. Slowly, Jessie's list grew. She found herself writing about things she'd taken for granted—the sun's warmth on her face, the taste of her mom's homemade cookies, and the quiet moments she spent drawing in her sketchbook.

Over the next few days, Jessie continued adding to her gratitude list. Whenever she felt a pang of envy or the urge to check social media, she reached for her notebook instead. She discovered that her life was filled with little joys she hadn't noticed before, moments that made her feel happy and content.

However, the real turning point came when Grace invited her to a small gathering at the local park. Jessie initially hesitated, worried that she'd feel out of place or that it wouldn't live up to the "perfect" moments she saw online. But she decided to give it a chance, focusing on being present rather than capturing the experience for social media.

When she arrived, she found friends sitting on a picnic blanket, laughing, and sharing snacks. There were no extravagant decorations or fancy outfits—just genuine smiles and a warm, welcoming atmosphere. Jessie relaxed, letting go of the pressure to "perform" or look a certain way. She was just there, in the moment, with people who accepted her as she was.

As the sun began to set, they all watched the sky turn shades of pink and orange. Jessie laughed, not because she had something clever to post or impress anyone, but because she genuinely felt happy. She didn't pull out her phone once, soaking in the experience instead.

That night, as she lay in bed, she realized that she hadn't thought about social media or what others were doing even once. She felt at peace, knowing her life didn't need to be a constant highlight reel. It didn't need to be filled with big, exciting moments to be meaningful.

Over the next few weeks, Jessie continued to practice gratitude. She spent less time on social media and focused instead on nurturing the relationships and experiences that genuinely mattered to her. She learned that just because her life didn't look like an Instagram feed didn't mean it wasn't valuable.

One afternoon, she sat with Grace, watching the clouds drift by. Grace looked over at her, a knowing smile on her face. "You seem different, Jessie. Happier, I think."

Jessie smiled, feeling the warmth of the sun and the contentment in her heart. "I am," she said softly. "I've realized I don't need to do what everyone else does. My life is good just the way it is."

As she sat there, surrounded by people who cared about her, Jessie felt grateful for the big moments and the quiet ones that didn't need to be posted or shared. She had learned to appreciate her journey, focus on what made her unique, and let go of the need to compare herself to others constantly.

Jessie had discovered that the cure to FOMO wasn't chasing after what everyone else had. It was finding joy in her own life, embracing the things that made her happy, and realizing she was enough just as she was.

CHAPTER SEVEN
Cancelled

Cancel Culture and Accountability

In today's digital world, cancel culture has become an influential yet controversial phenomenon. This chapter tackles the theme of cancel culture, exploring the consequences of social media backlash, the importance of accountability, and the journey of self-reflection and growth.

The story follows Isaac, a high school student who makes a thoughtless post online that quickly draws criticism from his peers. Within hours, he finds himself "canceled" by friends and classmates hurt or offended by his words. Isolated and confused, Isaac is forced to confront the impact of his actions. While initially defensive, he realizes the importance of empathy and taking responsibility for his mistakes. With guidance from a trusted teacher, Isaac learns to apologize sincerely, reflect on his actions, and grow from the experience. Rather than seeing himself as a victim, he understands that accountability is vital to personal growth. This chapter encourages readers to think critically about cancel culture, emphasizing the value of forgiveness, empathy, and the courage to learn from one's mistakes. It serves as a reminder that everyone is capable of change and redemption.

Isaac felt his phone vibrate in his pocket. He pulled it out to see dozens of notifications flashing across the screen. *New comments... New DMs... New mentions...* It was like a flood. His stomach churned with unease as he opened his messages, unsure of what he was about to see.

It only took a few seconds for reality to hit him. A single post he'd shared—a thoughtless, offhand joke—had somehow gone viral. What he'd meant as harmless humor was being called offensive, insensitive, and ignorant. He could feel his heart pounding as he scrolled through the angry comments on his feed.

"You're such a jerk, Isaac."

"Wow, I didn't know you were like this. Unfollowed."

"This is NOT okay. I hope everyone sees who you are."

Each comment stung like a slap to the face. Isaac had never been in this situation before and never imagined that his words could spark so much anger. He tried to tell himself it was just a joke, that people were overreacting. But the more he read, the harder it became to convince himself of that. Deep down, he knew he'd crossed a line—he just hadn't realized how serious it was until now.

The next day at school, the consequences were painfully apparent. People who used to greet him in the hallways avoided his gaze. His friends were distant, some even outright ignoring him. By lunchtime, he felt like he was invisible, sitting alone at a table that used to be crowded with laughter and chatter.

"Hey," he said, trying to join a conversation with his friend, Alex, who gave him a cold look and quickly turned away. Isaac felt a knot tighten in his chest. He'd never felt so alone, so completely shut out.

That evening, Isaac sat in his room, staring at the ceiling, guilt and shame gnawing at him. His initial defensiveness had faded, replaced by a nagging realization that maybe—just maybe—he was in the wrong. He picked up his phone and re-read his post, trying to see it through someone else's eyes. It wasn't funny, not in the way he'd thought. It was hurtful, dismissive of something he didn't fully understand.

He felt a wave of regret. He hadn't meant to hurt anyone, but his intentions didn't erase the impact of his words. He had made a mistake—a big one. And now, he was paying the price.

Isaac's mom knocked on his door and came in, her face soft with concern. "You've been quiet lately. Is something wrong?" she asked gently.

Isaac hesitated, then opened up about what had happened. He told her about the post, the backlash, and how he felt like he'd been thrown into a storm of anger he didn't know how to handle. His mom listened patiently, then put a reassuring hand on his shoulder.

"Isaac," she said, "we all make mistakes. What matters is how we respond to them. It sounds like you're learning something important from this, even if it's a painful lesson."

She encouraged him to reflect on his actions, to think about why people were hurt, and to consider what he could do to make things right. Her words lingered in his mind as he sat there, wondering how to fix what he'd broken.

The next day, he met with his school counselor, Mr. Thompson, who was always kind and understanding. Mr. Thompson welcomed Isaac into his office and listened as he poured out his worries, guilt, and confusion about what to do next.

"Isaac," Mr. Thompson said thoughtfully, "it sounds like you're realizing the power of your words. Everything we post can have a ripple effect, sometimes more than we realize. But learning from this experience is a form of growth. Mistakes don't define you, but how you handle them does."

Isaac nodded, feeling a glimmer of hope. "So... what should I do?" he asked.

Mr. Thompson suggested a path forward: to take responsibility and apologize, not in a quick, dismissive way, but with genuine sincerity. He also encouraged Isaac to take some time to learn more about the topic he'd joked about to understand why it was sensitive to others. "Empathy is the key," Mr. Thompson said. "Put yourself in their shoes."

That evening, Isaac wrote a heartfelt apology and posted it on his social media accounts. He didn't try to make excuses or downplay his actions. Instead, he acknowledged his mistake and explained that he was committed to learning and growing from this experience. He expressed genuine remorse, hoping that his words would show his sincerity.

To his surprise, some of his friends reached out with support. They appreciated his willingness to own up to his mistake. But others were still distant, and he understood that trust wasn't something he could regain overnight.

Over the next few weeks, Isaac made an effort to educate himself. He read articles, watched videos, and listened to stories from people affected by similar issues. The more he learned, the more he understood the pain that his joke had caused. He realized that words have weight and can wound just as much as actions.

Slowly, his relationships started to heal. His friends saw his changes, genuine remorse, and effort to improve. Isaac wasn't the same person he had been before; he was wiser, more thoughtful, and aware of the impact of his actions.

Alex approached him at lunch one day and said, "Hey, Isaac. Would you mind if I sat with you?"

Isaac nodded, grateful for the chance to rebuild a friendship he thought he'd lost. They talked, and Isaac felt a sense of peace for the first time since the incident. He had made amends, but more importantly, he had learned a lesson that would stay with him forever.

He understood accountability wasn't about punishment but growth, responsibility, and learning from mistakes. Through this experience, he discovered the importance of empathy, seeing the world through others' eyes, and using his voice to uplift rather than tear down.

In the end, Isaac emerged stronger, wiser, and with a more profound sense of social responsibility. He knew he couldn't undo what had happened but could control what he did moving forward. He promised himself to always think twice before hitting "Post" to remember that words carry power and that with that power came a responsibility he would never take lightly again.

CHAPTER EIGHT
Perfect Body, Perfect Lie

Body Image and Self-Acceptance

In a world where social media and pop culture constantly reinforce beauty standards, many teens feel pressure to attain an unrealistic "perfect" body. This chapter explores the theme of body image, the challenges of self-acceptance, and the journey toward embracing oneself beyond society's ideals.

The story follows Emma, a high school student constantly comparing herself to the images she sees online—photoshopped models, influencers with "perfect" bodies, and filtered pictures that portray an unattainable ideal. Over time, these comparisons affect her self-esteem, leaving her insecure and inadequate. She becomes obsessed with changing her appearance, trying to fit into a mold that isn't true to herself. Through conversations with a body-positive influencer and support from a caring friend, Emma begins questioning the standards to which she's been holding herself. She learns beauty isn't about meeting society's expectations but about feeling comfortable and confident in her skin. This chapter teaches readers the importance of self-love, self-acceptance, and finding beauty in their individuality rather than chasing a "perfect" image that is often nothing more than a lie.

Emma lay on her bed, staring at her phone as she scrolled through endless photos of flawless, smiling faces. Every image she saw seemed to taunt her, each a reminder of what she wasn't. Her feed was filled with influencers and models with the "perfect body"—flat stomachs, toned arms, and smooth, unblemished skin. Everyone looked effortlessly beautiful as if they were born to be perfect.

She caught herself staring at her reflection in the dark screen between scrolls, instinctively pulling her shirt over her stomach, hiding herself from her gaze. All she could see were the things she thought she needed to change. *Why couldn't she look like them?* She wondered if she'd ever be good enough or be able to look in the mirror and actually like what she saw.

The thought had nagged her for months since she started following those influencers. Every post about "healthy eating" and "toning workouts" made her feel guilty, as if she was somehow failing just by being herself. She tried every fad diet she came across, obsessed over her calorie intake, and started exercising daily, not because she enjoyed it but because she felt like she had to. She was chasing an image, a "perfect body" that she believed would finally make her happy. But the truth was, no matter what she did, she never felt any closer to that ideal.

Emma's friend Chloe came to study for an upcoming math test one afternoon. As they spread their notes across Emma's bed, Chloe noticed her friend's phone screen lighting up with yet another notification from an influencer's page.

"You follow way too many of those accounts," Chloe commented, shaking her head as she caught a glimpse of the perfectly posed photo on Emma's screen. "All those 'perfect' people… doesn't that get exhausting?"

Emma shrugged, trying to brush it off. "I just… I want to look like them, you know? They seem so happy and confident, and I… I don't."

Chloe frowned, her face softening with concern. "Emma, you're amazing just the way you are. Those photos aren't even real—they're edited and filtered. They're showing you what they want you to see, not what's real."

Emma bit her lip, feeling a pang of doubt. Part of her knew Chloe was right, but it was hard to shake the feeling that if she could achieve that "perfect body," everything would fall into place. She would be confident, happy, and finally feel good about herself.

Over the next few days, Chloe's words lingered in Emma's mind. She looked at her feed more critically, noticing things she hadn't seen before. The influencer with the sculpted abs had posted about "detox teas" she claimed were the secret to her figure, but Emma noticed the tiny disclaimer at the bottom of the post: #Ad. The girl with the perfect skin used heavy filters and carefully angled shots to hide her blemishes. Slowly, Emma began to see that maybe, just maybe, these images weren't as authentic as she'd thought.

One evening, as she was scrolling, she came across a post by a different kind of influencer. This woman wasn't promoting fad diets or perfect bodies. Instead, she talked openly about her struggles with body image, her journey to self-acceptance, and her mission to help others embrace their true selves. She posted photos that showed her as she was, without filters or edits, and her message was simple: *"You are enough, exactly as you are."*

The words struck Emma like a bolt of lightning. For the first time, she felt a sense of relief, like a weight was being lifted off her shoulders. She clicked on the woman's profile and found more posts filled with encouragement, self-love, and authenticity. Emma spent the next hour scrolling through her feed, reading stories from people who had been on a similar journey, people who had let go of the "perfect body" ideal and learned to embrace themselves.

Feeling inspired, Emma decided to make a change. She unfollowed all the accounts that made her feel bad about herself, replacing them with body-positive influencers who celebrated natural beauty and authenticity. She found resources and communities online dedicated to self-love and acceptance, and she began reading about how social media and society's unrealistic standards impact body image.

It wasn't easy, and the self-doubt didn't vanish overnight. But slowly, Emma started to feel a shift within herself. She began to approach exercise differently—not as a punishment, but as a way to feel strong and healthy. She chose foods that nourished her, not because she was trying to fit a specific size, but because she genuinely wanted to care for her body.

One afternoon, as she was working on a project for school, she glanced at herself in the mirror. For the first time in a long time, she didn't feel the immediate urge to criticize her reflection. Instead, she paused, taking in her features—the curve of her shoulders, natural smile, and unique beauty. She realized that she was starting to see herself differently, that the girl in the mirror was enough, exactly as she was.

Her newfound confidence didn't go unnoticed. Her friends noticed her standing a little taller, smiling a little brighter, radiating a quiet strength. Chloe, especially, was proud of her. "You seem... happy," she commented one day during lunch. "Like you're finally comfortable in your skin."

Emma smiled, feeling a warmth spread through her chest. "I am, Chloe. I am. I don't need to be anyone else. I need to be me."

As the weeks went by, Emma focused on her self-acceptance journey. She practiced gratitude for her body, appreciating it for all it did for her daily. She stopped comparing herself to others and began embracing her unique beauty, realizing she didn't need to fit anyone else's mold to be worthy or valuable.

One day, she decided to share her story on social media, hoping to reach others struggling with the same feelings she once had. She posted an unedited and unfiltered photo of herself with the caption: *"Learning to love myself has been the hardest but most rewarding journey. Remember to anyone struggling with body image: you are enough, just as you are."*

To her surprise, the post received an outpouring of support. Friends and strangers alike left comments, thanking her for her honesty, sharing their own stories, and expressing how much her words meant to them. Emma felt joy, knowing her journey could make a difference for others.

At that moment, she realized just how far she'd come. She no longer needed the approval of strangers on the internet to feel good about herself. She had found something more powerful—self-acceptance, resilience, and the courage to embrace her true self.

Emma's journey taught her that likes or comments didn't measure beauty. It came from within and grew stronger every time she accepted herself, flaws and all. She no longer chased the "perfect body" because she knew perfection was an illusion. What mattered was being happy, healthy, and true to herself.

And for Emma, that was the most beautiful thing of all.

CHAPTER NINE
The Overloaded Mind

Information Overload and Prioritization

In the age of the internet and constant connectivity, teens are bombarded with information from all directions—news, social media updates, notifications, and online content. This chapter explores the theme of information overload, focusing on the challenges of managing a constant stream of information and the importance of setting priorities to protect mental well-being.

The story centers around Caleb, a curious and intelligent student who loves staying informed. He spends hours scrolling through news feeds, watching videos, and staying up-to-date with everything happening worldwide. However, as Caleb's screen time increases, he feels overwhelmed, distracted, and anxious. His grades start slipping, and he needs help to focus on tasks that truly matter. Realizing the toll this endless flow of information is taking on his mental health, Caleb begins working with a school counselor to learn strategies for digital balance. Through mindful practices, prioritization techniques, and limiting screen time, Caleb learns to filter out unnecessary noise and focus on what aligns with his goals and values. This chapter emphasizes the importance of managing information intake, setting boundaries, and finding clarity in a world of digital distractions.

Caleb's day began like any other—with a buzz. His phone screen lit up, flooding his mind with notifications. News headlines, social media updates, group chat messages, and endless notifications from every app he'd downloaded. He hadn't even climbed out of bed, but his brain was racing to process everything around him. He felt as if he couldn't miss a single thing or he'd fall behind.

Caleb was known among his friends as "the encyclopedia," who always knew the latest updates about… everything. Whether it was a global event, the newest trend, or a meme, Caleb was the go-to guy. He enjoyed feeling informed, as if being on top of all the latest news gave him some edge. But lately, it had started to feel like too much. The information he used to love now weighed on him, filling his mind like a bucket overflowing with water.

At school, it became harder to concentrate. During class, he'd find himself distracted, thinking about something he'd read that morning or itching to check his phone for updates. His grades began to slip, and his teachers noticed that he wasn't as focused as he used to be. Caleb tried to ignore it, but the stress only grew. He was torn between his love of staying informed and the overwhelming noise that seemed to clutter his mind constantly.

One afternoon, as he sat in the school library attempting to finish an assignment, he was utterly distracted again. His phone buzzed for the hundredth time, and he instinctively reached for it. But before he could check it, a hand reached out and gently placed itself on his screen, blocking his view.

"Caleb," his best friend, Jade, said, frowning. "You've got to stop. You're addicted to that thing."

He sighed, looking down at his phone, feeling embarrassed and frustrated. "I know, but… I want to stay informed. There's so much going on, and I don't want to miss anything."

Jade gave him a sympathetic look. "But at what cost? You're so wrapped up in everything that you're not paying attention to what's right in front of you. It's like your mind is stretched thin."

Caleb considered her words, feeling the truth in them. His mind was on constant overdrive, unable to settle or rest. He was so used to consuming information nonstop that he didn't know how to stop. But maybe… maybe he needed to.

The next day, Caleb visited the school counselor, Ms. Rivera. He'd heard from other students that she was understanding and might be able to help him find a way to cope. He shared his struggles with her, admitting how overwhelmed he felt by the never-ending stream of information.

Ms. Rivera listened carefully, nodding as she considered his words. "Caleb, it's wonderful that you're curious and want to stay informed. But there's something called 'information overload.' When we take in too much information without giving our minds a chance to process it, it can lead to stress, anxiety, and, as you're experiencing, difficulty focusing on what matters."

Caleb nodded, feeling relieved in knowing that his struggle had a name. "So… what do I do? I don't want to be out of the loop, but I don't want to feel like this anymore."

Ms. Rivera offered him a warm smile. "It's all about setting boundaries and prioritizing. Here are a few things you could try. First, choose specific times to check your phone rather than constantly checking throughout the day. That way, you're not distracted when focusing on something else. Second, consider limiting your sources. Instead of following dozens of news outlets and accounts, pick a few reliable ones and trust them to keep you updated."

Caleb took her advice, realizing that it sounded simple but effective. He could stay informed but didn't need to be tuned in every second of the day. He also decided to try Ms. Rivera's suggestion to do a "digital detox"—a period without his phone entirely.

Over the weekend, he started his detox. It was hard at first. He reached for his phone out of habit, feeling missing something crucial. But he resisted the urge, reminding himself that the world would still be there even if he didn't check in every second.

He spent his time doing things he hadn't done in a while—he read a book, went for a walk without music blasting in his ears, and even spent time with his family without checking his phone every few minutes. At first, it felt strange, like he was disconnected. But slowly, he felt a sense of peace he hadn't experienced in a long time.

On Monday, he returned to school feeling refreshed. His mind felt more straightforward and less cluttered, and he could focus on his classes in a way he hadn't in weeks. He was fully present in his surroundings for the first time.

Jade noticed the change immediately. "You seem... different," she said with a smile. "Did you finally take a break from that phone?"

Caleb grinned, nodding. "I did. And you were right, Jade. I needed this. It's nice not to be overwhelmed by everything going on."

From that point on, Caleb began setting boundaries with his digital life. He limited himself to checking news updates once in the morning and once in the evening, freeing up his day for more important things. He unfollowed accounts that made him anxious or pressured to keep up, focusing instead on reliable sources and positive influences.

He even started practicing mindfulness, which Ms. Rivera suggested to help him manage his thoughts. When he felt the urge to check his phone, he'd take a deep breath and ground himself in the present moment. Over time, he learned to appreciate the value of living in the here and now rather than being constantly plugged into the endless stream of information.

Caleb's grades began to improve as he regained his focus. More than that, he felt a new control over his mind. He no longer felt like being pulled in a hundred directions, lost in a sea of notifications and headlines.

One afternoon, while hanging out with Jade, he looked at the sunset, a vibrant mix of oranges and pinks, and realized he hadn't even thought about reaching for his phone to take a picture. He was... enjoying the moment.

"Thank you," he said to Jade, who gave him a curious look. "To help me realize that I don't need to know everything all the time. I needed that wake-up call."

Jade smiled, nudging him playfully. "Well, I'm glad you finally listened! Life's too short to spend it glued to a screen."

Caleb laughed, feeling a warmth in his chest that he hadn't felt in a long time. The world was still full of information and things he'd never known, but that was okay. He'd found a way to balance his curiosity with his peace of mind, focusing on what mattered.

Ultimately, Caleb learned he didn't need to know everything, be everywhere, or see everything. Sometimes, just being present was enough. And with that realization, he found a sense of calm he'd been searching for all along.

CHAPTER TEN
The Real Me

Embracing Authenticity in a Filtered World

In a society where social media often highlights only the best moments, many teens feel pressured to present a "perfect" version of themselves, hiding their true selves behind filters and carefully curated posts. This chapter explores the themes of authenticity, self-acceptance, and the courage to show one's true self in a world that often values perfection over honesty.

The story follows Zara, a high school student known for her perfectly curated Instagram feed. To her followers, she seems to have it all—great friends, exciting adventures, and a flawless appearance. However, Zara feels increasingly disconnected from her authentic self behind the screen. Tired of constantly maintaining an image that doesn't reflect her reality, she takes a bold step: sharing her unfiltered self. With vulnerability and courage, Zara begins posting photos and stories showing her authentic experiences, including the ups and downs, imperfect moments, and genuine feelings. As she embraces her authenticity, Zara realizes that people connect more with her authentic self than her filtered image. This chapter inspires readers to embrace their uniqueness. It shows them that authentic connections and self-worth come from being genuine to themselves, not from trying to live up to others' expectations.

Zara stared at her phone screen, scrolling through her Instagram feed, each photo perfectly arranged to fit her carefully curated aesthetic. Pastel colors, soft lighting, and every smile meticulously posed. She'd spent hours editing these photos, making sure each looked flawless, projecting the image of a life she thought others would admire.

Her feed was popular; people commented on how "perfect" her life looked. She'd become known as "that girl with the beautiful Instagram," and she loved the attention at first. But over time, the pressure to maintain that illusion had grown unbearable. Her real life didn't feel anything like the images on her screen. The bright, smiling Zara on Instagram was a far cry from the girl who often felt anxious and overwhelmed in her day-to-day life.

She was exhausted. Each post felt like another layer of a mask she wore, hiding the parts of herself she was afraid to show. She never posted the days when she felt lonely or when her anxiety left her too drained to get out of bed. No one knew about her struggles in school, the fights with her parents, or the insecurities she felt every time she looked in the mirror. They only saw the filtered version of her life, the parts she allowed them to see.

One evening, as she lay in bed, Zara felt frustration wash over her. She was tired of pretending and living two separate lives: the real one, filled with ups and downs, and the picture-perfect one she posted online. She wanted to show people the real her—the Zara who had bad days, sometimes cried herself to sleep, and didn't always have it together. But she was afraid. What if people didn't like the honest Zara? What if they saw her vulnerabilities and judged her?

That night, she took a deep breath and decided it was time for a change. She opened Instagram and hesitated momentarily before switching to her photo library. She selected a picture she'd never planned to share—one of herself sitting on her bedroom floor with no makeup, her hair messy, and her eyes puffy from crying. It wasn't glamorous or "Instagram-worthy," but it was real. It was her.

With her heart pounding, she began typing a caption:

"Life isn't always perfect, and neither am I. For a long time, I've hidden the struggles behind a filter, pretending everything's okay when it's not. This is the real me. Some days are hard, and that's okay. I'm learning to be okay with being imperfect. Here's to being real."

She pressed "Post" before she could second-guess herself, her heart racing as the notification confirmed her post was live. She felt exposed and vulnerable, like standing in front of a crowd with nothing to hide behind. But at the same time, she felt a strange sense of relief. For once, she wasn't pretending. She was showing people the truth.

Almost immediately, her phone buzzed with notifications. Comments began pouring in, and Zara braced herself, fearing judgment or criticism. But as she read each comment, her fear turned into surprise and gratitude.

"Thank you for sharing this, Zara. I needed to see this."

"You're so brave for being honest. I've struggled too, but I couldn't talk about it."

"This is beautiful, Zara. You're inspiring so many people by being real."

She couldn't believe it. Instead of judging her, people were reaching out, sharing their struggles, and thanking her for vulnerability. She realized she wasn't alone—so many others felt the same pressures, hid behind filters and perfect pictures, and felt like they had to live up to impossible standards.

Over the next few weeks, Zara's Instagram became a different space. She still posted photos, but they were real—moments of joy and sadness, success and failure, highs and lows. She shared stories of days when she felt confident and didn't. She opened up about her struggles with anxiety, the pressures she felt to be "perfect," and her journey toward self-acceptance.

Her followers responded with overwhelming support, many sharing their stories, grateful for a space where they could be authentic without fear of judgment. Zara had built a community based on authenticity, a space where people could come together to share their struggles, support each other, and remind each other that it was okay not to have it all together.

One day, a friend from school, Ava, approached her in the hallway. "Hey, Zara. I just wanted to say… your posts have helped me. I always thought you had this perfect life, and it made me feel like I was failing. But seeing you be real… made me feel like I didn't have to pretend either."

Zara smiled, feeling a warmth in her chest. "Thank you, Ava. I was scared to be open, but connecting with people has been amazing. I think we all deserve to be real with each other."

Ava nodded, her eyes shining with appreciation. "You've inspired a lot of us to embrace our true selves. It's like… you permitted us to be imperfect."

Zara realized then that being real didn't just benefit her—it helped others, too. By allowing herself to be vulnerable, she'd given others the courage to do the same. She'd created real connections that weren't based on filters or perfection but on honesty and understanding.

As Zara continued her journey, she noticed a shift in herself. She felt lighter, more at peace with who she was. She no longer needed to hide behind a mask or pretend to be someone she wasn't. She was free to be Zara—flawed, authentic, and human.

For the first time, she felt like she was enough. The pressure to be perfect was lifted and replaced by a deep self-acceptance. She didn't need the validation of likes or followers to feel good about herself; she knew her worth came from within.

In the end, Zara's journey taught her that natural beauty wasn't about fitting into a perfect mold or hiding behind filters. It was about embracing every part of herself—the good, the bad, the messy, and the beautiful. She learned that authentic connections were built not through perfection but through honesty, vulnerability, and the courage to show up as herself.

She felt proud as she scrolled through her feed, filled with natural, unfiltered moments. Her Instagram was no longer a display of perfection but a true reflection of her real life—imperfect yet rich with meaning, connection, and authenticity. Zara had found her authentic self and knew she would never return to the filtered lie.

CHAPTER ELEVEN
Fitting In vs. Standing Out

Peer Pressure and Individuality

In high school, the desire to fit in is often intense, and many teens feel pressured to conform to their peers' expectations and norms. However, this chapter explores the theme of individuality, highlighting the importance of embracing one's unique identity and staying true to oneself, even in the face of peer pressure.

The story centers on Michael, a student who has always tried to fit in, even if it means going along with things he doesn't believe in. Surrounded by friends who value appearances, trends, and popularity over authenticity, Michael feels increasingly lost and disconnected from who he truly is. He thinks that his true interests and personality are buried under the weight of others' expectations. Through self-reflective moments and encounters with a mentor encouraging him to embrace his individuality, Michael realizes that standing out is more valuable than simply fitting in. He starts to pursue his true passions and stands up for his beliefs, discovering that true friends will appreciate him for who he is. This chapter encourages readers to resist the pressure to conform, embrace their unique qualities, and find empowerment in authenticity.

Michael had always been "that guy" in his friend group—the one who went along with whatever was popular, even if it wasn't his thing. He wore the same trendy clothes, listened to the same music, and joined in on the latest fads, even if he secretly thought they were ridiculous. His friends were the kind who measured self-worth in likes, followers, and brand names, and while it wasn't exactly his style, Michael went along with it—fitting in felt safer, even if it meant hiding parts of himself.

But lately, he felt like something was missing. Whenever his friends talked about the latest fashion trends or the most popular influencers, he zoned out, thinking about things he genuinely cared about. Like his love for drawing and his fascination with art history—things he had never discussed with his friends. He'd never shown anyone his sketchbook, afraid they'd laugh or brush it off as "uncool."

One day, while scrolling through social media, Michael stumbled upon a video of a street artist painting a mural. Mesmerized, he watched as the artist brought colors and shapes to life on a wall, transforming it into something beautiful and unique. Michael felt a spark within him, a reminder of his love for art. He realized how long it had been since he'd drawn anything for himself without worrying about what others might think.

Later that week, his friends were planning to attend a concert for a band they all pretended to love because it was popular. Despite not caring for the music, Michael always went along with these outings. But this time, something held him back. He felt a pull toward something more authentic, a desire to reconnect with his interests. "Hey guys, I think I'm gonna sit this one out," he said, surprising even himself with the words.

His friends exchanged glances, clearly taken aback. "What? Come on, man, it's going to be awesome!" one of them said, nudging him. But Michael shook his head, determined to do something different, even if he couldn't quite explain it to them.

Instead of attending the concert, he spent the evening drawing for the first time in months with his sketchbook. He felt a surge of happiness as he lost himself in his art, free from the need to fit into anyone else's mold. For once, he was doing something that felt right to him and came from within.

As the days went by, Michael started making small changes. He didn't go out of his way to follow the latest trends and stopped pretending to be interested in things he didn't care about. He even started bringing his sketchbook to school, cautiously doodling during breaks, letting pieces of himself show in little ways.

At first, his friends noticed and made casual remarks, poking fun at his new "weird" habits. But Michael was determined not to let it bother him. The more he embraced his individuality, the more he realized that true friends would accept him for who he was, not for his role in their social circle.

One day, in art class, his teacher announced an upcoming art exhibition for students to showcase their work. Michael felt a mix of excitement and fear. Part of him wanted to participate, but he wasn't sure he was ready to show the world his sketches. Yet something in him—the exact part that had kept him from the concert and encouraged him to draw again—urged him to leap.

With a deep breath, he signed up.

As the exhibition approached, he poured himself into his work, creating pieces that reflected his thoughts and feelings. He used colors that spoke to him, lines that conveyed emotions he'd never shared with anyone. When he looked at his finished pieces, he felt a sense of pride, knowing they were indeed his, free from anyone else's expectations.

The night of the exhibition, he stood beside his artwork, nervously watching as people walked by. His friends showed up, and he first braced himself, expecting them to tease him. But as they looked at his work, their expressions softened. They seemed genuinely impressed.

"Wow, Michael, I didn't know you were into art," one of his friends said, sounding surprised but sincere.

Michael smiled, feeling a wave of relief. "Yeah, it's something I've always liked. I just… never showed anyone."

Another friend nodded. "These are amazing. You should do more of this."

Standing there, Michael realized that his friends' reactions didn't matter as much as he'd thought. For the first time, he felt indeed seen

—not for the clothes he wore or the music he listened to, but for who he was. And the best part was that he liked who he was.

After that night, Michael continued to embrace his individuality. He found that he was happier, more confident, and more comfortable in his skin. He spent more time with people who shared his interests and started forming connections based on genuine interests, not just convenience.

Of course, some friendships changed, and a few faded away. But he didn't mind. He understood now that it was better to have a few trustworthy friends who accepted him for who he was than a crowd of acquaintances who only liked the version of him that fit their mold.

Michael's journey taught him that fitting in wasn't as valuable as he'd thought. Embracing his unique qualities gave him a new sense of empowerment and freedom. He discovered that true friends would stand by him, not because of how well he blended in, but because of the natural person he was becoming.

In the end, Michael learned that the courage to stand out was far more valuable than the comfort of fitting in. And as he continued to grow, he found peace knowing that authenticity was his greatest strength, a gift he would never again hide behind the mask of conformity.

CHAPTER TWELVE
Behind the Mask

Mental Health Awareness and Stigma

Mental health struggles can often be hidden behind a mask of smiles, humor, and outward confidence, especially among teenagers who fear judgment or don't want to seem vulnerable. This chapter explores the theme of mental health awareness, highlighting the importance of breaking down stigma and encouraging openness and support for struggling people.

The story follows Lily, a cheerful and outgoing student known for her positivity and friendly personality. But behind her smiles, Lily hides her struggles with depression and anxiety, feeling ashamed and afraid to open up to others. She worries that people won't understand or might think differently of her if they knew about her inner battles. Eventually, her mental health challenges become too heavy to bear alone, and she reaches out to a trusted teacher who connects her with a school counselor. With support and guidance, Lily opens up about her feelings to her friends and family, discovering that seeking help is a sign of strength, not weakness. This chapter emphasizes the importance of mental health awareness, breaking the silence around mental health issues, and fostering a supportive community that understands and accepts individuals for who they are beyond the masks they wear.

Lily had always been known as the girl with the biggest smile. In the hallways, she greeted everyone with a cheerful wave, and she was the one cracking jokes in class, making her friends laugh. To everyone around her, Lily seemed like the epitome of happiness. But no one knew that behind that infectious smile, she was fighting a battle no one could see.

Every morning, she'd look in the mirror and practice her smile until it felt right. Then she'd leave her room, greeting her parents, friends, and teachers as if everything were OK. No one noticed the exhaustion in her eyes or the heaviness she carried in her heart. She had become an expert at pretending, at wearing her mask so well that not even her closest friends suspected anything was wrong.

But as the days went by, the mask became harder to wear. Her sadness grew heavier, making it harder to get out of bed, concentrate, and keep up with the cheerful facade everyone expected from her. At night, she'd lie in bed staring at the ceiling, feeling trapped in her mind, the silent ache pressing down on her. She wanted to talk to someone, to tell someone what she was going through, but every time she thought about it, a voice inside her whispered, *They won't understand. They'll assume you're weak.*

One day, as she was sitting in math class, trying her best to focus, she felt the walls closing in on her. Her chest tightened, and her hands shook. She excused herself and hurried to the bathroom, locking herself in a stall, her heart racing as she struggled to breathe. She sat on the cold tile floor, feeling helpless and alone, the reality of her isolation crashing down on her.

As she returned to class, her teacher, Ms. Turner, noticed her pale face and red-rimmed eyes. Ms. Turner had always been one of Lily's favorite teachers—a warm, understanding woman who always seemed to know when something was wrong. As Lily gathered her books to leave that day, Ms. Turner gently touched her shoulder. "Lily, would you mind staying for a few minutes after class? I want to talk to you."

Lily nodded, feeling dreadful. As the other students filed out, Ms. Turner closed the door and gestured for Lily to sit down.

"Lily, I just wanted to check in with you," Ms. Turner said softly, her eyes filled with concern. "You're usually so upbeat, but lately... I've noticed you seem a bit distant. Are you okay?"

Lily's heart pounded, and she felt the familiar urge to put on her mask, to brush it off with a smile and a quick reassurance. But something about Ms. Turner's kindness made her pause. She took a shaky breath, feeling the words rise in her throat, words she'd held back for so long.

"Actually… I'm not okay," she whispered, her voice barely audible. "I feel… I'm drowning, but no one can see it."

Ms. Turner reached out, placing a comforting hand on Lily's. "Thank you for telling me, Lily. I can only imagine how hard it must be to carry this alone. You don't have to go through this alone. Have you thought about talking to someone—a counselor, maybe?"

Lily shook her head, tears welling up in her eyes. "I was scared. I didn't want anyone to know. I didn't want people to think I was weak or… broken."

Ms. Turner smiled gently. "Lily, asking for help doesn't make you weak. It takes strength to admit when you're struggling. Mental health is as important as physical health; everyone needs support sometimes."

Hearing those words felt like a small weight lifting off her chest. She nodded, realizing for the first time that maybe it was okay to ask for help and that she didn't have to keep pretending.

With Ms. Turner's encouragement, Lily made an appointment to meet with the school's mental health counselor, Mr. Jenkins. Sitting in his cozy office, surrounded by calming colors and soft music, Lily felt a nervous flutter in her stomach. But as she began talking to Mr. Jenkins, she felt a surprising sense of relief, like she was finally releasing all the emotions she'd bottled up for so long.

Mr. Jenkins listened without judgment, offering her a safe space to express her fears, sadness, and the pressure always to be "happy Lily." He helped her understand that depression was not something to be ashamed of, that it was a common struggle, and that there were ways to manage it. He taught her breathing exercises to calm her anxiety and suggested she start journaling her thoughts, a way to process her emotions without feeling overwhelmed.

With each session, Lily felt herself growing more robust. She began opening up to her friends, explaining why she sometimes needed time alone or couldn't always be the "life of the party." To her surprise, her friends didn't judge her; they supported her, offering her understanding and kindness.

One day, she decided to share a part of her journey with her classmates. In a social studies presentation about mental health, Lily stood before the class, her heart pounding, and shared her story. She spoke about the pressure to be perfect, the stigma around mental health, and how seeking help had changed her life.

"I used to think asking for help was a weakness," she said, her voice steady. "But I learned it's one of the bravest things you can do. If you are struggling, please know you're not alone. Some people care and want to help you."

As she finished, the room was silent. Then, one by one, her classmates began to clap, a few wiping away tears. Several students approached her afterward, thanking her for her honesty, sharing their struggles, and telling her how much her words meant to them.

At that moment, Lily realized that she hadn't just helped herself by taking off her mask—she'd also helped others. She saw that being vulnerable wasn't a weakness but a strength, a way to connect with others on a deeper level. She no longer felt the need to pretend or hide her pain. She was learning to accept herself, flaws and all.

Over time, Lily smiled again, a genuine smile from a place of self-acceptance. She continued her sessions with Mr. Jenkins, working through her ups and downs, but she no longer felt ashamed. She was proud of her journey, her courage to seek help, and her story's impact on others.

Lily's journey wasn't perfect, and there were still difficult days. But she knew that she wasn't alone, that she had people who cared, and that she had the strength to keep moving forward. She'd learned to embrace herself, both the happy and challenging moments, knowing that every part of her journey was valid.

Ultimately, Lily discovered true happiness wasn't about wearing a mask or pretending to be perfect. It was about being honest, being vulnerable, and allowing herself to be supported. She learned that by removing her mask, she could finally show the world her true self— and that self was worthy of love and acceptance, just as she was.

CHAPTER THIRTEEN
Disconnected in a Connected World

Social Isolation and Building Real Connections

In a time when social media and online platforms allow people to stay "connected" 24/7, it's paradoxical that many teens still feel lonely and isolated. This chapter delves into the theme of social isolation, exploring the difference between virtual connections and meaningful, in-person relationships and the importance of building real, supportive friendships.

The story centers around Jaden, a high school student with hundreds of friends online who spends most of his free time in virtual spaces— chatting, gaming, and using social media. Despite his digital connections, Jaden feels lonely, realizing his relationships lack depth and true companionship. Yearning for real friendships, he decides to step out of his online comfort zone and join a club at school. Through engaging in face-to-face activities, sharing experiences, and bonding with classmates in the real world, Jaden begins to understand the value of genuine connections. This chapter encourages readers to look beyond the screen, seek deeper, real-life relationships, and find the courage to build friendships that provide proper support, trust, and understanding.

Jaden's phone buzzed beside him, lighting up with a new notification. It was from one of his many online friends, a guy he'd met in a gaming chatroom, inviting him to join an online tournament that evening. Jaden glanced at the message, his thumb hovering over the screen to quickly type "Yes." But instead, he hesitated.

Despite having hundreds of online friends, Jaden felt lonelier than ever. Most of his day was spent scrolling through social media, chatting in group messages, and gaming with people he'd never met. He knew everything about his friends' avatars and favorite game strategies but barely had anyone to call a real friend at school. Outside the virtual world, his life felt empty.

The realization struck him during lunch a few days earlier. As usual, Jaden sat alone, eating while scrolling through his phone. A group of classmates sat nearby, laughing and chatting, and he noticed one of them playfully pushing the other. Jaden felt a pang of envy. It had been so long since he'd laughed with someone face-to-face, without a screen in between.

He thought about how easily he could chat with his online friends about anything, yet he could barely muster up the courage to talk to someone new in his school. It was strange—he felt connected to so many people through his devices, yet he had never felt so alone.

That evening, Jaden sat at his desk, looking around his room. Posters of his favorite video games covered the walls, and his gaming setup shone neon lights. Usually, this was his comfort zone, his escape from the pressures of the real world. But tonight, it felt... different. He felt restless like something was missing.

Sighing, he logged onto the gaming platform and started playing the tournament. His team was winning, but he couldn't focus. He barely enjoyed it anymore. The screen felt like a barrier, a wall keeping him from the real world. He longed to experience things firsthand, to feel the energy of honest conversations and laughter that didn't come from pixels on a screen.

The next day at school, Jaden noticed a poster on the hallway bulletin board advertising the school's photography club. They met every Thursday, it read, and were looking for new members. Jaden's heart skipped a beat. Photography had always interested him, but he'd never considered joining a club. He was always too busy with online tournaments and social media. But maybe this was his chance to try something new.

After school, he went to the photography club room, feeling excited and nervous. As he stepped in, a few students were gathered around, talking and laughing, each holding cameras. They looked up as he entered, offering friendly smiles.

"Hey! Are you here for the photography club?" one of the girls asked, waving him over.

Jaden nodded, trying to calm his nerves. "Yeah... I, uh, thought I'd check it out."

The club members welcomed him warmly, and the teacher in charge, Mr. Alford, explained that they planned a photography outing in the park over the weekend. Jaden felt excitement—it would be his first time participating in an activity like this outside the confines of his screen. He agreed to join them, hoping this could be the beginning of something real.

That Saturday, Jaden met the group at the park. Armed with cameras and notebooks, they wandered through the greenery, snapping pictures of flowers, trees, and birds. Jaden found himself lost in the moment, enjoying how he could capture the world's beauty without needing a filter or an edit. He chatted with his clubmates as they shared tips on angles and lighting, laughing at each other's attempts to get the perfect shot.

By the end of the day, he felt lighter and happier than he had in a long time. Being there, in person, surrounded by people who shared his interests, made him feel alive in a way his online connections never had.

As the weeks passed, Jaden continued to attend the photography club meetings, building genuine connections with his new friends. He found himself slowly stepping away from his online world, spending less time gaming and more time experiencing life firsthand. He went to the library with his clubmates, attended school events, and joined them for lunch.

One day, as he sat in the cafeteria with his new friends, laughing over an inside joke, he felt a sense of belonging he hadn't felt in years. It wasn't about followers or likes or the number of friends in a chatroom. It was about real, human connections that made him feel seen and valued.

When his phone buzzed in his pocket with a message from his gaming group, Jaden didn't feel the usual urge to respond immediately. He smiled, realizing he didn't need to live behind a screen. He still enjoyed gaming and chatting online, but it was no longer the center of his life. He'd found something better, something real.

Over time, Jaden learned the value of balance. He didn't have to give up his digital friends or his love for gaming, but he didn't have to be defined by them. He could enjoy the virtual world while also being fully present in his real one. In that balance, he found a new sense of happiness.

As he continued to explore photography, Jaden discovered that life wasn't about curating a perfect image online—it was about capturing moments that mattered, both in front of and behind the camera. It was about being present, making memories with real people, and building relationships beyond pixels and screens.

Jaden had finally stepped out of his digital bubble, embracing the messy, beautiful, natural world around him. And in doing so, he found the connection he'd been searching for all along.

CHAPTER FOURTEEN
Too Much, Too Fast

Burnout and Time Management

In the high-achieving world of modern teens, many students feel pressured to take on as much as possible—academics, extracurriculars, volunteer work, and social commitments. This chapter explores the theme of burnout, emphasizing the importance of time management, balance, and prioritizing well-being over constant productivity.

The story follows Nia, a driven student involved in sports teams, academic clubs, honors classes, and volunteer work. She's known as a "go-getter," but Nia feels overwhelmed and exhausted beneath the surface. As her responsibilities pile up, she struggles with fatigue, stress, and declining grades, unable to keep up with the relentless pace she's set for herself. With guidance from her school counselor, Nia learns the importance of setting boundaries, prioritizing her commitments, and incorporating self-care into her routine. She discovers that it's okay to say no and that her worth isn't defined by how busy she is. This chapter teaches readers the value of balance and mindful time management, encouraging them to focus on what truly matters and nurture their mental health.

Nia stared at her planner, her eyes darting across the countless scribbles and sticky notes that filled every square inch of her week. Honors classes, soccer practice, debate club, volunteering at the animal shelter, tutoring, and student council... there wasn't a single free hour left. Most people would feel accomplished looking at such a packed schedule, but all Nia felt was exhaustion.

The worst part was that she couldn't figure out how it had gotten so overwhelming. She used to love each of these activities. They were what made her... her. Being an honors student, the star athlete, the dependable friend—those were the things she prided herself on. But somewhere along the line, the excitement had faded, replaced by a nagging sense of dread each time she looked at her planner.

Every night, she stayed up later, desperately trying to finish assignments or prepare for the next day's obligations. Sleep had become a luxury she couldn't afford, and her grades, once stellar, began to slip. Her teachers noticed. Her parents noticed. But whenever someone asked her if she was okay, she forced a smile, pretending everything was fine. After all, Nia had always been the one who could handle anything.

One Friday after school, as she was heading to another club meeting, Nia's favorite teacher, Mrs. Collins, caught her in the hallway. "Hey, Nia, can I talk to you for a minute?" she asked, her tone gentle but concerned.

Nia nodded, trying to hide her tiredness. Mrs. Collins guided her into an empty classroom and pulled up a chair next to her.

"Nia," she began, her voice soft, "I've noticed you've been looking a little worn out lately. I know you have a lot on your plate. Are you doing okay?"

Nia bit her lip, her eyes falling to her hands. She wanted to say that everything was fine, that she was just a little tired, but the words wouldn't come. She'd been holding it all in for so long that, finally faced with someone who cared, she felt a wave of emotion welling inside her.

"I… I don't know," she whispered, her voice barely audible. "I feel like I'm drowning. There's so much to do, and I don't know how to keep up."

Mrs. Collins nodded, her expression understanding. "You're doing so much, Nia. You're trying to be everything to everyone, and that's a lot of pressure. Have you considered talking to the school counselor? She might be able to help you figure out how to manage everything without feeling so overwhelmed."

Nia hesitated. She'd never considered seeing the counselor before. It felt like admitting defeat like she couldn't handle things alone. But deep down, she knew she couldn't keep going like this. With a nod, she agreed.

The following week, she sat in the school counselor's office, pouring out her worries to Mrs. Rivera, the counselor. Mrs. Rivera listened patiently as Nia described her packed schedule and the pressure to excel in everything. She admitted that she feared letting people down and not meeting everyone's expectations.

"Sometimes, Nia," Mrs. Rivera said gently, "we put so much pressure on ourselves because we think we must do it all. But part of growing up is learning when to say no and understanding that you don't have to do everything to be valued. You're allowed to take a step back."

Nia stared at her, feeling a mixture of relief and fear. The idea of saying no, of stepping back, was foreign to her. She had always been the girl who could handle it all, who thrived on being busy. But as she thought about it, she realized it was time to prioritize her well-being.

Mrs. Rivera handed her a blank sheet of paper. "Let's try something. Please write down everything you're involved in, and then we'll review it together and determine what's truly important to you. You might find that not everything needs to stay on this list."

Nia took a deep breath and began writing. As she filled the page with all her activities, responsibilities, and obligations, her list grew longer and longer. When she was finished, Mrs. Rivera looked it over.

"Alright," Mrs. Rivera said, "let's go through each one. Please think about why you're doing each of these things. Is it because you love it, or do you feel you must?"

As they went through the list, Nia realized something surprising. Some of the activities she'd been dedicating so much time to weren't things she genuinely enjoyed anymore. She'd been doing them. She felt obligated because she didn't want to disappoint anyone or thought they'd look good on her college applications.

By the end of the session, Nia had crossed off several activities from her list. It wasn't easy—she felt a pang of guilt with each one—but she also felt a sense of relief, like a weight had been lifted.

Mrs. Rivera smiled at her. "Remember, Nia, it's okay to take care of yourself. You're not letting anyone down by setting boundaries. In fact, by focusing on what truly matters to you, you'll be able to give those things your best effort without feeling so overwhelmed."

Over the next few weeks, Nia implemented her new plan. She resigned from several clubs, told her soccer coach she needed to cut back on practices, and even turned down a classmate's tutoring request. At first, it wasn't easy. She worried about what people would think, about whether they'd see her as less capable.

But gradually, she started noticing a difference. She wasn't as exhausted and began enjoying her remaining activities more. With a less packed schedule, she had time to breathe, relax, and do things she loved just for the sake of it. She found herself reading books, drawing, and spending time with friends without feeling rushed to the following commitment.

Her grades improved, too. With more time to focus on her schoolwork, she could study without the constant stress of trying to cram everything in. She no longer felt like she was on the verge of burnout; instead, she felt balanced and in control of her time and life.

One day, she ran into Mrs. Collins in the hallway, and her teacher smiled. "You look happier, Nia," she said. "I'm glad to see you taking care of yourself."

Nia smiled back, feeling proud. She'd learned a valuable lesson—that her worth wasn't tied to how many activities she could juggle or how much she could accomplish in a day. She was more than her achievements, and it was okay to prioritize her well-being.

As she continued through the school year, Nia said no more often, setting boundaries that allowed her to maintain a healthy balance. She realized that she didn't have to be everything to everyone and that taking care of herself made her a better student, friend, and person.

In the end, Nia discovered that life wasn't about doing it all—it was about doing what mattered most and giving her best effort. She had found her balance, and in doing so, she'd found herself.

CHAPTER FIFTEEN
Real Friends, Real Support

Friendship and Support Networks

Friendships are crucial in shaping one's experiences and sense of belonging in high school. However, finding genuine friends who offer support and understanding can be challenging. This chapter explores the theme of friendship, highlighting the importance of having a support network and the strength that comes from leaning on others and being there for them in return.

The story follows Alyssa, a student who believes she has to handle her struggles alone, not wanting to burden others with her problems. She keeps her challenges to herself, thinking she should be strong and independent. However, as her stress and worries build up, she feels isolated and overwhelmed. When a close friend notices Alyssa's struggles and reaches out, she finally opens up, realizing that true friends are there to listen and support each other. Through this experience, Alyssa learns that asking for help is a sign of strength, not weakness, and that support networks are vital for emotional resilience. This chapter encourages readers to appreciate real friendships, showing that true friends stand by each other through the highs and lows, offering compassion, understanding, and support when needed.

Alyssa sat alone in the library, staring at the open textbook before her, though she hadn't read a word. Her mind was somewhere else, tangled in a mess of thoughts and worries that weighed her down like stones. She felt utterly overwhelmed by the demands of school, the pressures of her family's expectations, and the mounting list of things she needed to get done. But more than anything, she felt alone.

It wasn't that she didn't have friends. Alyssa had a group of people she hung out with at lunch, people she laughed with and spent time with in class. But she'd never been able to shake the feeling that she had to face her problems alone. She was scared to open up, to show the messy parts of herself that she kept hidden beneath her composed exterior. She didn't want to burden anyone with her problems.

She often thought, *Why would anyone want to hear about my issues? Everyone else seems to have it all together.* She was afraid of being judged or, worse, pitied. So she smiled and pretended that everything was fine, even as she felt herself sinking deeper into stress and loneliness.

One afternoon, as she was packing up her things to leave the library, her friend Mia caught up to her. "Hey, Alyssa! I haven't seen you much lately. Everything okay?"

Alyssa forced a smile. "Yeah, just... you know, busy with school and stuff."

Mia looked at her, her brow furrowing slightly. "You've seemed a bit... off. I mean, you don't seem like yourself. Are you sure everything's alright?"

Alyssa hesitated, feeling a lump form in her throat. She wanted to tell Mia everything—she felt overwhelmed, was scared of failing, and didn't feel good enough. But the words wouldn't come. She managed another weak smile. "I'm fine."

Mia didn't press further, but her concerned expression lingered as they parted ways. As Alyssa lay in bed, Mia's words replayed in her mind that night. She hadn't realized how much she'd been holding in and shutting herself off from the people who cared about her. She wondered if she might not have to handle everything alone.

The next day, as she walked into school, Mia approached her again. This time, she didn't ask if Alyssa was okay. Instead, she said, "Let's hang out after school. I'll treat you to coffee. My treat."

Alyssa wanted to decline, to hide away in her shell as she always did, but something inside her urged her to accept. She nodded, managing a small smile. "Okay."

After school, they headed to a cozy coffee shop nearby. As they sipped their drinks, Mia started talking about her struggles with school and family pressures, opening up about things Alyssa had never known. "Sometimes, I feel like I'm carrying this huge weight," Mia admitted. "But I realized it gets a little easier when I talk about it, you know? Just knowing someone else understands."

Hearing Mia's honesty, Alyssa felt a surge of relief. Maybe she wasn't as alone as she'd thought. She took a deep breath and, for the first time, began to open up about her struggles. She told Mia about the overwhelming pressure, the sleepless nights spent worrying, and the constant fear of not measuring up.

Mia listened without interrupting, her expression filled with understanding and compassion. When Alyssa finished, Mia reached across the table and squeezed her hand. "Alyssa, you don't have to go through this alone. I'm here for you. We all are. Friends are supposed to support each other."

The weight on Alyssa's chest lifted just a little. She hadn't realized how much she'd needed to share to let someone else see the real her. For the first time in a long time, she didn't feel like she was fighting her battles alone.

Over the next few weeks, Alyssa made an effort to let her friends in, little by little. She started sharing bits and pieces of her struggles with her close friends, opening up about her stress and fears. And to her surprise, they responded with kindness and support. They offered encouragement, checked in on her, and even made her laugh when needed.

She realized she wasn't a burden to them; they wanted to be there for her, just as she'd always been there for them. Alyssa had been afraid of appearing weak for so long, but she discovered that vulnerability wasn't weakness—it was a sign of trust and strength.

One day, when Mia was going through a rough time with her family, Alyssa offered support. She listened, comforted Mia, and reminded her she wasn't alone. It felt good to be there for her friend, to return the kindness and empathy that Mia had shown her.

In time, Alyssa understood that friendships weren't one-sided; they were two-way streets where both could offer and receive support. Real friends didn't judge or pity—they stood by each other, lifting each other through the highs and the lows.

As she embraced the power of her support network, Alyssa felt her resilience grow. Although she faced challenges, she no longer felt like she had to bear them alone. She had a circle of people who cared, understood, and would stand by her no matter what.

By the end of the school year, Alyssa had become more comfortable opening up to her friends and leaning on them when things got tough. She no longer needed to hide behind a mask or pretend to be perfect. She knew she could be herself—messy, flawed, and genuine—and her friends would still be there.

Alyssa learned that life wasn't meant to be faced alone. It was meant to be shared with people who cared and were willing to help carry the load when things got heavy. By accepting their support, she realized she was creating a stronger, more meaningful bond with them.

In a world that often encouraged independence and self-reliance, Alyssa found strength in connection. She found courage in vulnerability and discovered that real friendship meant allowing others to be there for her, just as she was there for them.

Through her journey, Alyssa learned that genuine support didn't just mean standing by someone in the good times but walking with them through the challenges, fears, and struggles. She no longer felt alone because she had friends by her side every step of the way. And she knew that whatever challenges came her way, they would face them together, with the power of real friends and genuine support.

Chapter 16:

The Invisible Wall

Social Anxiety and Building Confidence

For many teens, social anxiety can feel like an invisible wall, keeping them from fully engaging with others and enjoying their high school years. This chapter explores the theme of social anxiety, highlighting the internal battles many face and the journey to build confidence and overcome fear in social settings slowly.

The story centers on Lena, a high school student with intense social anxiety. She often feels like an outsider, struggling to join clubs, participate in class, or make new friends. She avoids social gatherings and dreads group projects, feeling trapped and isolated by her insecurities. With the help of a supportive teacher and gentle exposure exercises, Lena begins to take small steps to confront her fears. She practices speaking before a minor, understands the group, learns calming techniques, and gradually builds self-confidence. Through her journey, Lena discovers the power of resilience and self-acceptance, realizing that bravery is about taking small steps, even when uncomfortable. This chapter encourages readers to embrace their journey, showing that overcoming social anxiety is possible with patience, support, and self-compassion.

Lena tugged at her sleeves as she walked through the crowded hallway. The noise was overwhelming—the hum of conversations, the slamming of locker doors, the laughter, and the teasing that echoed around her. It all blended into a whirlwind of sound, and every step she took felt heavier than the last. She kept her eyes glued to the floor, hoping she could slip through without being noticed if she avoided looking at anyone and being invisible felt safe.

Lena wasn't a part of any clubs, she didn't go to any games, and she'd managed to dodge every invite she'd ever received to a friend's house. Social events and group activities felt like unbearable obstacles to her, things to be avoided at all costs. The thought of trying to talk to people or, even worse, making friends filled her with a deep sense of dread.

But this year, things were getting more challenging. Her teachers had started assigning more group projects, and Lena couldn't avoid the anxiety that washed over her every time she had to work with classmates. In every group, she felt like she didn't belong, like a burden or an afterthought. She wanted so badly to participate, to make friends, but the invisible wall of her anxiety always kept her at a distance.

One day, after Lena had avoided yet another group activity, her homeroom teacher, Ms. Rivera, approached her gently after class. Ms. Rivera had always been kind, noticing the little things about her students. She saw how Lena stayed quiet, avoided others, and seemed to disappear into the background. She knew Lena needed support but understood that pushing her too hard would worsen things.

"Lena, I wanted to talk to you for a minute," Ms. Rivera said, her voice soft and warm. "I've noticed that you seem uncomfortable with group activities. How are you feeling about things?"

Lena hesitated, feeling her chest tighten. She wanted to shrug it off, just saying she was fine and leaving. But Ms. Rivera's kind eyes made her feel safe enough to let down her guard just a little.

"It's... hard," Lena admitted, her voice barely above a whisper. "I don't feel like I belong. It's like... I'm always on the outside, watching everyone else."

Ms. Rivera nodded, understanding in her gaze. "Social situations can be challenging for a lot of people. You're not alone in feeling this way, Lena. But I think you can start feeling more comfortable with some small steps. It doesn't have to be all at once. Just little steps."

Lena looked down, fidgeting with her hands. She wasn't sure if she could manage even a small step. But Ms. Rivera's words gave her a tiny glimmer of hope.

Over the next few weeks, Ms. Rivera introduced Lena to "exposure exercises." They were small, manageable tasks that allowed her to confront her fears without overwhelming herself. The first one was simple: sit at a table in the library with other students, even if she didn't talk to anyone. Lena's heart pounded the entire time, but she pushed through. It felt uncomfortable, but she felt a slight accomplishment when she finished.

Gradually, the exercises increased. The following week, Ms. Rivera encouraged her to say hello to one person she didn't know. Lena's stomach churned at the thought, but she mumbled a shy "hi" to a girl from her math class. The girl smiled back and said hello, and for the first time, Lena felt a sliver of connection—a tiny crack in the invisible wall she had built around herself.

Ms. Rivera continued to guide Lena, celebrating every small victory and helping her understand that progress didn't have to be perfect; it just had to be consistent. Lena started to keep a journal, writing down each small win and every step she took outside of her comfort zone. With each entry, she could see her progress and felt proud.

Eventually, Lena felt confident enough to join a club—Photography Club, something she'd always been interested in. She thought it would be easier since she could focus on taking photos, which didn't require her to be the center of attention. At her first meeting, she felt the familiar nerves creeping up, but she pushed them aside. She took her camera, introduced herself to a few members, and snapped photos.

The other members welcomed her warmly, appreciating her unique style and how she saw the world through her camera lens. Slowly, Lena began to make friends in the club. She was part of something for the first time, and it felt good. She was no longer standing on the sidelines, watching others connect. She was building connections of her own, one click of the camera at a time.

One day, she even volunteered to present a slideshow of her photos to the club. Standing before her new friends, her voice shook as she explained her pictures, but they listened intently, offering supportive smiles and clapping when she was done. Lena had done something she never thought possible—she had broken down the invisible wall, if only for a moment, and let herself be seen.

Through these small victories, Lena realized that social anxiety didn't define her. She could work through her fears and find her voice, even if it took time. She learned courage wasn't the absence of fear but the willingness to face it, one step at a time.

With Ms. Rivera's help and determination, Lena began believing in herself. Her journey wasn't over, and there would still be difficult days. But she now knew that she was capable of overcoming her fears. She understood that every small step counted, and with each step, she was building her confidence, breaking down the walls, and finding her way in the world.

Lena smiled as she looked around the room, surrounded by friends and classmates who saw her for who she was. She was no longer invisible, which felt like the most significant victory.

Chapter 17:

The Weight of Expectations
Parental Pressure and Self-Discovery

Balancing parental expectations with personal aspirations is challenging for many teens. This chapter explores parental pressure and the inner conflict between fulfilling family dreams and pursuing one's passions.

The story follows Raj, a diligent high school student whose parents envision him as a future doctor or engineer. However, Raj's true passion lies in filmmaking, and he spends his free time writing scripts and experimenting with a camera. Fearing his parents' disapproval, he hides this side of himself. Over time, the pressure and disconnect from his true self build up, making him feel stifled.

With encouragement from a supportive teacher, Raj gathers the courage to converse honestly with his parents. He shares his passion for filmmaking, helping them understand his commitment. Through this journey, Raj learns to balance his family's expectations with his dreams, highlighting the importance of open communication and self-discovery. This chapter emphasizes finding a path that aligns with family respect and personal fulfillment.

Raj sat in his room, staring at the textbooks across his desk—physics formulas, biology notes, math exercises—all waiting for him to dive in. The clock ticked by, but he couldn't focus. His mind wandered back to his parents' voices from that morning.

"You have to be the best, Raj. Only the best make it to medical school. You know how important this is for our family," his father had said, his tone more stern than supportive. His mother had nodded along, echoing the expectations placed on him for as long as he could remember.

In his parents' eyes, becoming a doctor was more than a career; it was a dream they'd had for him since he was a child. They'd sacrificed so much to give him a better life, moving to a new country, working long hours, and pushing him to excel academically. Raj understood their sacrifices, and he loved them for it, but the weight of their expectations pressed down on him like an unrelenting force.

He opened his notebook and tried to focus, but his eyes drifted to his sketchbook underneath his textbooks. Drawing had always been his secret passion, where he felt free. He loved creating characters, landscapes, and abstract designs that came alive in his imagination. But he knew his parents wouldn't understand. To them, art was a secondary hobby, distracting from his "real" future.

After another half-hearted attempt to study that evening, Raj found himself drawn to his sketchbook. He pulled it out and began sketching a scene lingering in his mind—a sunrise over a mountain, symbolizing the feeling of hope and freedom he craved. As he drew, he felt a release, a calmness that he couldn't find in his schoolwork. For those few moments, he felt like he was indeed himself.

The next day at school, Raj's art teacher, Ms. Collins, noticed him doodling on the corner of his notebook. She'd seen him drawing before, and she'd always been impressed by his talent. After class, she gently approached him.

"Raj, I noticed you're quite talented with your drawings. Have you ever thought about pursuing art seriously?" Ms. Collins asked with a smile.

Raj hesitated. "I... I love drawing, but it's just a hobby. My parents want me to focus on academics to become a doctor."

Ms. Collins nodded understandingly. "I understand. But you know, following your passion has a lot of value. Art isn't just a hobby—it's a way to express who you are. You have a gift, Raj. Don't be afraid to explore it."

Her words stayed with him for days. Part of him wanted to ignore them, to push his passion aside and focus on his studies. But another part of him—the part that came alive when he was sketching—

yearned to explore his artistic side, to discover what he was truly capable of.

The internal struggle grew stronger. The pressure to meet his parents' expectations clashed with his desire to pursue art. He felt caught between two worlds, each pulling him in opposite directions. One evening, while scrolling through his favorite art website, Raj came across a local art competition. The theme was "Dreams and Aspirations." The thought of entering excited him, but the fear of disappointing his parents held him back.

With a mixture of hesitation and courage, he secretly entered the competition. For the next few weeks, he poured his heart into his piece, depicting a young person standing at a crossroads with paths leading to different dreams and futures. It reflected his own life, a way to channel his conflicting emotions.

The night before the competition, he finished his piece and stood back, admiring his work. For the first time, he felt a sense of accomplishment entirely his own. This was his art, his expression, his truth.

The day of the competition arrived, and Raj's nerves were through the roof. He attended the exhibition in a nearby gallery, surrounded by other young artists and their families. His heart pounded as he saw people admiring his work, some even taking photos. When the judges announced the winners, Raj held his breath.

"Third place goes to Raj Patel for 'Crossroads of Dreams.'"

The applause around him felt surreal, and for a moment, he was overcome with pride and validation. But that feeling was quickly overshadowed by the realization that his parents had no idea he was here or about his secret passion and hidden achievement.

That evening, Raj returned home with a small plaque and a bittersweet feeling. He wanted to tell his parents but didn't know how they'd react. Taking a deep breath, he approached them in the living room.

"Mom, Dad… I need to talk to you."

His parents looked up, surprised by the severe tone of his voice. He took out the plaque and showed it to them, explaining the competition and how he had been exploring art. His mother's eyes widened, and his father's face was confused and disappointed.

"Raj, we didn't come all this way for you to become an artist," his father said. "We have big plans for you, giving you a stable future."

Raj took a deep breath, feeling the weight of their expectations press down on him again. "I know, Dad. And I appreciate everything you've done for me. I do. But… art is important to me. It's a part of who I am."

His mother looked at him with worry. "Raj, we just want what's best for you."

"I understand," he replied gently. "But I think what's best for me is finding a balance. I can still study hard, but I want to pursue art, too. I don't want to give up a part of myself to meet expectations."

After a long, emotional conversation, his parents began to see that art was more than a passing hobby for Raj—it was his passion. While they didn't fully understand, they agreed to let him explore it as long as he kept up with his academics.

With their reluctant support, Raj felt a newfound freedom. He began to work on finding balance, dedicating time to his studies, and pursuing art. He started sharing his artwork with friends and teachers, finding encouragement and support. He felt like he was finally breaking free from the weight of expectations and discovering who he indeed was.

Ultimately, Raj learned he didn't have to choose between his parents' dreams and his own. By setting boundaries, having honest conversations, and embracing his passions, he could honor his family while being true to himself. For the first time, he felt light, as if the weight of others' expectations had lifted, leaving room for his dreams to grow.

And that, he realized, was the most critical path he could ever take.

Chapter 18:

The Digital Shadow
Privacy and Online Reputation

In today's digital world, every post, comment, and photo leaves a trace that forms a person's digital shadow. This chapter explores the theme of privacy and online reputation, highlighting the importance of responsibly managing one's online presence.

The story follows Zoe, a lively high school student who enjoys sharing her life on social media. She posts photos, shares updates, and comments freely, assuming that her online activity is harmless. However, things turn when one of her impulsive posts is misinterpreted and shared widely. Suddenly, Zoe's reputation is questioned, impacting her relationships at school and even her plans.

Through this experience, Zoe learns the power of her digital shadow and the importance of protecting her online reputation. With guidance from a mentor, she begins to make thoughtful decisions about what she shares online. This chapter emphasizes the lasting impact of digital actions, teaching teens to consider privacy and responsibility to safeguard their future.

Zoe was always online. Her social media accounts were filled with vibrant photos of her life—selfies with friends, snapshots of vacations, and moments captured at parties. She loved sharing her experiences and connecting with people. To her, social media was a way to express herself and feel connected, even to people she barely knew.

One evening, Zoe received a notification that changed everything. An anonymous account had tagged her in a post—a picture of her at a party, but she didn't even remember being captured in a moment. But this wasn't just any photo. It was one she'd never have shared herself, one that showed her in a way that could easily be misinterpreted. The caption was mocking, loaded with insinuations about her character and lifestyle.

At first, she brushed it off. "People know me," she thought. "They'll understand that it's just a joke." But as the hours passed, comments started flooding in, and not all were kind. Some people she didn't even know began tagging others, adding to the mockery. People she'd never met were commenting on her character, judging her based on a single, poorly timed image.

She felt humiliated. Her phone kept buzzing with notifications, each one adding to her anxiety. She tried turning off her notifications, but curiosity kept pulling her back to the post. She wanted to know what people were saying, but each comment only made her feel worse. Friends she thought she could trust liked the post or left laughing emojis as if her dignity was a joke for everyone else to share.

Zoe found herself sinking into a pit of shame and insecurity. At school, she felt like everyone was watching her, whispering about her. She avoided eye contact, kept her head down, and skipped lunch to avoid the cafeteria crowds. Her once vibrant social life had become a dark cloud of paranoia and self-doubt.

After a few days of hiding, she confided in her older brother, Nick. She hadn't told her parents—she felt they wouldn't understand, and they might even judge her for the photo. But Nick was different. He was only a few years older and had gone through his social media dramas.

"Nick," she started hesitantly. "Something happened online, and I don't know what to do. It's like… everyone's against me. They're making fun of me over this one picture, and it feels like I'll never live it down."

Nick listened, his expression serious. "Zoe, the internet can be harsh, and people quickly judge based on what they see in a split second. But it's important to remember that this isn't the world's end. You're more than one picture, and this will pass. People have short memories online."

"But what if they don't forget? It's like… my whole reputation is ruined over this," Zoe said, her voice breaking.

Nick took a deep breath. "I get it. I do. I've been there, and it's terrible. But I learned a few things that helped me get through it. First, you need to take control of your online presence. Don't let anyone else define you."

Zoe felt a glimmer of hope. "What do you mean by 'take control'?"

"Start by reaching out to the people who matter—your close friends. Explain the situation to them and ask for their support. If they're true friends, they'll understand and stand by you. Then, block the anonymous account that posted the photo and report it. If they continue to harass you, get your school involved or even consider legal action if necessary."

Zoe nodded, feeling a bit more empowered. "I guess I didn't think about reporting it. I was too focused on the embarrassment."

"And remember," Nick continued, "you can also share posts representing who you truly are. Show people that there's more to you than this one moment. If people see the real you, they'll never forget that one bad picture."

With Nick's support, Zoe started taking small steps to regain control. She contacted her closest friends and explained how the photo affected her. Most were understanding, and a few even apologized for not realizing how serious it was. They offered to report the post to her, which made her feel less alone.

Next, Zoe reported the photo and blocked the account. She felt relieved, knowing she wouldn't see any more cruel comments or likes on that post. It didn't erase the damage, but it was a start.

Over the following weeks, Zoe became more mindful of her social media presence. She began to share posts that showcased her genuine interests—photos from her art club, moments volunteering at an animal shelter, and glimpses of her love for nature. Slowly, people started to see her as more than just the party girl they thought they knew.

Zoe also took time to reflect on her relationship with social media. She realized she had been too focused on how others perceived her rather than embracing her true self. Social media had become a performance, and she was ready to change that.

As she regained confidence, she became more cautious about what she shared online. She set her profiles to private and began thinking twice before posting anything. She learned that privacy was a form of self-respect and that she didn't owe anyone a window into every aspect of her life.

One day, while scrolling through her feed, Zoe noticed a new comment on one of her art photos. It was from a girl in her art class who she barely knew: "I love this painting! You're so talented, Zoe."

Zoe smiled. She had genuinely rebuilt her reputation. Her friends appreciated her for who she was, not for the filtered, flashy image she once thought she had to project.

The digital shadow of that old post still lingered in her mind, but it no longer defined her. She had learned to control her narrative, focus on her life's natural connections, and protect her privacy. Zoe's journey taught her that reputation can be fragile in the digital age, but resilience and authenticity can rebuild it more vital than ever.

Most importantly, Zoe discovered that she was more than the sum of her social media posts. Her worth was defined by her character, passions, and genuine relationships with those around her—not by the likes, comments, or photos that once seemed so important.

She logged off that day with a lighter heart, grateful for the lesson she'd learned and the strength she had gained.

Chapter 19:

The Path Less Taken
Career Pressure and Exploring Alternative Paths

Many teens feel pressured to follow expected routes, like becoming doctors, lawyers, or engineers, in a society that often emphasizes traditional career paths. This chapter explores the theme of career pressure and encourages teens to consider alternative paths that align with their true passions.

The story follows Ethan, a high-achieving student whose family has always envisioned him pursuing a stable career in finance. However, Ethan's passion lies in woodworking and craftsmanship—an interest far removed from his family's career expectations. Although he tries to conform, Ethan feels unfulfilled and disconnected from his true self.

With support from a school career counselor, Ethan starts exploring career opportunities in design and craftsmanship. Slowly, he gains the courage to share his dreams with his family. This chapter highlights the importance of pursuing one's passion, even if it means taking the less traveled path, and reminds readers that success can come from making alternative, fulfilling career choices.

Ethan was known as the "smart kid" in school. Teachers praised him, friends admired him, and his family was proud. He was good at science and math, excelling in subjects everyone said were the keys to a successful career. Everyone assumed he would become a doctor, an engineer, or a scientist. He'd heard the word "prestigious" so many times that he couldn't remember when he didn't associate his future with it.

But as college application season approached, Ethan felt a strange dread. The thought of pursuing the conventional, "prestigious" career paths his parents dreamed of didn't excite him. Instead, it filled him with a heavy feeling of unease. While he was good at math and science, he didn't have the passion for them he saw in others. Secretly, Ethan had always wanted to be a writer.

For as long as he could remember, he'd written stories in the back of his notebooks, creating worlds and characters, pouring his thoughts and dreams onto paper. Writing was his escape, his comfort zone, where he felt truly alive. But he held back whenever he considered telling his family or friends about his dream. "Writing isn't a real career," he'd heard people say. "You'll never make a living from it."

One evening, Ethan sat at his desk, staring at his college applications. Each one listed a science or engineering major, the path that seemed expected of him. His fingers hovered over the keyboard, and a familiar sense of anxiety crept in. He knew he was filling out the forms for everyone else, not for himself.

He decided to take a break and opened a story he'd been working on. Within moments, he was lost in the world he'd created. For an hour, he forgot about college applications, expectations, and societal norms. At that moment, he realized how deeply he loved writing and how it made him feel like his true self. But could he abandon everyone's expectations and pursue it?

Ethan found himself in the guidance counselor's office the next day at school. Ms. Carter had been his counselor since his first year, and she knew him well. Sensing his restlessness, she asked, "Ethan, you seem troubled. Are you feeling uncertain about college?"

Ethan sighed, rubbing his temples. "It's not that I don't want to go to college… it's just… I'm not sure I want to go for the reasons everyone expects. Everyone thinks I should be a doctor, engineer, or something scientific. But I'm not excited about that. I just… I don't know how to tell my parents I want to be a writer."

Ms. Carter smiled, her eyes warm with understanding. "Ethan, college is about finding your path, not fulfilling someone else's expectations. And while practical careers are important, so are passion and purpose. Writing is as valuable as any other career if it brings you joy."

Ethan looked down, hesitant. "But… I'm scared they'll think I'm wasting my potential. I don't know if they'll ever understand."

Ms. Carter leaned forward, her tone gentle but firm. "You'll never know unless you're honest with them. Besides, you're not saying you won't be successful; you want to define success on your terms. Life isn't a one-size-fits-all journey. You must find what fulfills you, not what makes others happy."

Those words stayed with Ethan long after he left the counselor's office. That night, he sat down with his parents, heart pounding, hands trembling, and told them everything. He explained his love for writing, his desire to pursue a career in storytelling, and his decision not to go into science to please others.

His parents listened, their faces unreadable. His father finally broke the silence. "Ethan, we always thought you'd be a doctor or engineer. You're so talented in those fields."

Ethan nodded, swallowing hard. "I know, Dad. And I'm grateful for your belief in me. But writing is what makes me feel alive. I want to pursue it seriously and believe I can make a difference with my words."

After a lengthy discussion, they agreed to support him, though they admitted it would take time to adjust to the idea. They didn't fully understand his passion, but they loved him enough to let him find his way. The relief that washed over him was immense; he had taken his first step toward his path.

In the following months, Ethan started exploring ways to turn his passion for writing into a viable career. He attended writing workshops, connected with mentors, and even started a blog where he shared his stories and experiences. His blog began to gain followers, and people appreciated his unique voice and perspective. He realized that there was an audience for his words, and his confidence grew.

Ethan also explored other options, like journalism, copywriting, and content creation, understanding that there were multiple ways to sustain a career in writing. He didn't have to be limited to traditional paths or preconceived notions of success. He could create his own.

As graduation approached, Ethan felt a renewed sense of purpose. His friends were surprised when he announced that he majored in English and creative writing. "I thought you were going to be an engineer or something," one of his friends said, clearly baffled.

Ethan smiled, feeling a weight lift from his shoulders. "That was everyone else's dream for me. I've decided to follow my own."

By the end of high school, Ethan had found his passion and learned to stand up for it. He had broken free from the pressure to conform and embraced the less-taken path. His journey reminded him that sometimes, the most tremendous success isn't achieving someone else's dreams but having the courage to pursue your own.

And as he looked ahead, Ethan knew that the road might be challenging, uncertain, and filled with obstacles. But he also knew that it was his road, his journey, which made all the difference.

Chapter 20:

A New Beginning
Resilience and Moving Forward

Life can bring unexpected challenges, and building resilience is critical to overcoming adversity and finding a fresh start. This chapter explores the theme of resilience, focusing on the courage to move forward despite setbacks.

The story follows Emma, a high school student who has recently experienced a difficult family situation that has turned her world upside down. Once a vibrant, active student, Emma feels lost and unmotivated, her confidence shaken. She struggles to engage with school and her friends, feeling weighed down by her circumstances.

With the support of a compassionate teacher and a close friend, Emma gradually begins to rediscover her inner strength. She learns to cope with her emotions and rebuild her confidence through journaling, setting small goals, and participating in activities that bring her joy. This chapter highlights Emma's journey to resilience, inspiring readers to find hope in difficult times and embrace each new day as a chance for growth and renewal.

As the final semester of high school ended, the campus buzzed with the excitement of graduation. Students were busy planning their next steps, discussing their dreams, ambitions, and life beyond high school. For Emma, the anticipation was bittersweet.

Emma had always been one of those students who wore a smile on her face, even when things were tough. She was known for her optimism and her warm personality. But behind her cheerful exterior, Emma had been struggling with her mental health for years. Anxiety, low self-esteem, and bouts of depression were battles she fought silently, afraid of burdening others with her struggles. She kept herself busy with school activities and friendships and maintained good grades, hoping she wouldn't have to confront the feelings gnawing at her from within if she kept moving.

As graduation approached, the pressure seemed to mount even higher. Her friends talked about college and ambitious plans for the future, but Emma felt like she was standing on shaky ground. While everyone else seemed so sure of themselves, she was unsure if she had the strength to make it through. The uncertainty and fear of entering a world that demanded even more responsibility weighed heavily on her heart.

While wandering the school hallways one afternoon, Emma ran into Ms. Morales, her guidance counselor. Ms. Morales was always attentive, occasionally checking in with Emma throughout the school year. Sensing Emma's hesitation, she invited her into her office for a chat.

"Emma, I can tell something's on your mind," Ms. Morales said gently, looking at her with kind eyes. "Graduation is a big milestone, but it's okay to feel uncertain about what comes next."

Emma hesitated, not sure if she was ready to open up. But something about Ms. Morales's warm and non-judgmental expression encouraged her. Slowly, she began to share her fears, feelings of inadequacy, and the weight of expectation pressing down on her. For the first time, she admitted that she didn't have everything figured out.

Ms. Morales listened patiently, nodding along. When Emma finished, she spoke in a calm, reassuring voice. "Emma, you're not alone in feeling this way. Many students are unsure what they want to do, and that's okay. Life isn't a race, and there's no set timeline you have to follow. Sometimes, the most important thing is just taking one step at a time."

Emma felt a glimmer of relief but still felt uncertain. "But everyone else seems so sure of themselves. I feel like I'm falling behind and don't know where to start."

Ms. Morales smiled. "You're not falling behind, Emma. The truth is that everyone has their struggles, even if they don't show them. And remember, growth doesn't happen overnight. It's a journey. You're strong, and I believe in you. And most importantly, you need to believe in yourself."

With Ms. Morales's encouragement, Emma started to feel a renewed sense of hope. She realized that she didn't have to have everything planned out. She just needed to trust herself and take things one day at a time.

Over the next few weeks, Emma began focusing on small steps that helped her feel more grounded. She started journaling, reflecting on her experiences and emotions, and setting realistic, achievable goals. One of her goals was to actively care for her mental health—something she had previously ignored in the hustle of school life. She also began meditating, taking walks in the park, and practicing self-care meaningfully.

Her friends noticed the subtle changes in her demeanor. She was still the same optimistic Emma but had a new depth. She was more present, more at ease with herself, and less caught up in the pressures of fitting in. As she became more comfortable in her skin, Emma realized she didn't need to live up to anyone else's expectations. She could define her path and her success.

As graduation day loomed, Emma decided to open up to her close friends about her struggles. She was nervous at first, fearing that they might not understand. But to her surprise, her friends listened compassionately and even shared their challenges and insecurities. Many also had anxieties about the future, self-doubt, and pressure to succeed.

"I never would have guessed," one friend admitted, her voice filled with empathy. "I always thought you had everything together, Emma. I'm so glad you shared this. It makes me feel less alone."

At that moment, Emma realized the power of vulnerability. By opening up about her struggles, she had helped her friends feel comfortable with their uncertainties. They formed a stronger bond, rooted in mutual understanding and support, ready to face the future together.

On graduation day, Emma stood proudly in her cap and gown, her heart brimming with gratitude. She looked around at her classmates, each on their unique journey, facing their struggles and triumphs. She knew the road ahead would have its challenges, but she felt ready, equipped with resilience, self-awareness, and the knowledge that she wasn't alone.

As she received her diploma, Emma felt a surge of pride—not because she had it all figured out, but because she had found the courage to face herself, accept her vulnerabilities, and take life one step at a time. The path ahead was still uncertain, but she was ready to embrace it with open arms.

At that moment, Emma understood that graduation wasn't just the end of high school—it was the beginning of a new chapter where she could walk her path, define her happiness, and continue growing in ways she had never imagined.

And with that, she walked off the stage, a new sense of confidence and clarity blossoming. The journey was beginning, and she knew she had the resilience to keep moving forward no matter what came her way.

Made in the USA
Columbia, SC
14 November 2024

4e8f7b75-8fdc-4783-b7f8-227c55531f6eR01